Minds on **Mathematics**

Minds on **Mathematics**

Using **Math Workshop** to Develop ·

Deep Understanding in Grades 4–8

WENDY WARD HOFFER

HEINEMANN
Portsmouth, NH

Heinemann
361 Hanover Street
Portsmouth, NH 03801–3912
www.heinemann.com

Offices and agents throughout the world

The author and publisher wish to thank those who have generously given permission to reprint borrowed material:

Excerpts from *Common Core State Standards* © Copyright 2010. National Governors Association Center for Best Practices and Council of Chief State School Officers. All rights reserved.

Library of Congress Cataloging-in-Publication Data
Hoffer, Wendy Ward.
   Minds on mathematics : using math workshop to develop deep understanding in grades 4–8 / Wendy Ward Hoffer.
       pages   cm
   Includes bibliographical references.
   ISBN-13: 978-0-325-04434-7
   ISBN-10: 0-325-04434-1
   1. Mathematics—Study and teaching (Middle school). 2. Group work in education.   I. Title.
QA20.G76H64 2012
510.71'2—dc23   2012021746

Editor: Katherine Bryant
Production: Vicki Kasabian
Cover and text designs: Monica Ann Crigler
Cover photographs: Lisa Fowler and Laura Mahoney
Typesetter: Valerie Levy, Drawing Board Studios
Manufacturing: Steve Bernier

Printed in the United States of America on acid-free paper
16   15   14   13   VP   2   3   4   5

For my children, infinitely.

The greater danger for most of us
lies not in setting our aim too high and falling short
but in setting our aim too low and achieving our mark.
—Michelangelo

Contents

Acknowledgments

This book is in your hands thanks to all of the teachers, students, colleagues, friends, and family who've taught me about thinking and understanding. I am especially grateful to:

My own teachers: Mrs. Britt, who knew about differentiation; Mr. Cypher, who blew our ten-year-old minds with systems of equations; Mrs. Silber, who let me out of a lockstep math curriculum; Mr. Gunther, who pushed us all; Dr. Andrew Garrod, who taught us how to record classroom learning without passing judgment; Dr. Mike Atkin, who modeled the critical role of joy in any teaching endeavor.

All of my students and colleagues at Educo Adventure School, Green Acres School, Hillview Middle School, Rocky Mountain School of Expeditionary Learning, the Odyssey School, University of Denver, and Regis University for their energy and honesty.

The Public Education & Business Coalition (PEBC) for the opportunity to be a part of an amazing community of thinkers: Rosann B. Ward for supporting the expansion of PEBC's work to serve math and science teachers and learners, as well as encouraging me in all of my endeavors; our foremothers Ellin Oliver Keene, Cris Tovani, Judy Hendricks, and more for their dedication to finding new ways to meet students' needs; Denise, Natalie, Lori, Jon, and Francie for everything you do behind the scenes.

Moker Klaus-Quinlan for starting our expeditionary playgroup and getting me my first gig with the PEBC, being a challenging and devoted thinking partner, generously sharing her insight on math teaching and learning, and offering up her carefully scripted classroom observations, several of which appear in this book. And for helping me to avoid wearing cross-country ski attire to professional events.

Suzanne Plaut for always asking, "To what end for students?" cultivating my thinking about how to best support math and science teachers, blessing the launch of the PEBC Math Institute, encouraging me as a writer, editing countless versions of these chapters, and introducing us to hot water with lemon. Above all, for giving me room to run.

My colleagues on the Ed Team: Paula Miller for her artful ability to articulate what we do, and her expansive vision of what is possible; Annie Patterson for her insight into the authentic needs of teachers, dedication to students, and laughter; Mindy Armbruster for running all the numbers and keeping our feet on the ground; Jennifer Bell for looking after all the details, including making sure I have something to eat; Manon Scales, for tackling any task—including polishing this book's bibliography and test-driving the problems in Appendix B—with exquisite attention to detail, and a smile.

PEBC lab hosts for sharing amazing thinking and courage with teacher guests every year. Especially, Rachel Rosenberg, Angie Zehner, Tracey Shaw, and Deb Maruyama for the incredible work they do with learners every day that inspires teachers to expect more from students.

PEBC project schools, teachers, administrators, and students for their experimentation with and feedback on many of the ideas presented in this book, including: Adams City High School, Harrington Elementary School, (former) John Dewey Middle School, Prairie Middle School, Preston Middle School, Thornton Middle School, Shelby County High School, Shelby East Middle School, Shelby West Middle School, Skinner Middle School, Tascosa High School.

Those teachers who granted me permission for their stories and work to appear in this book, including Jeff Cazier, Michael Dennis, Suzanne Guelda, Ryan Martine, Deb Maruyama, Rachel Rosenberg, Tracey Shaw, Brad Smith, Donna Whitis, and Angela Zehner, and their students.

Katherine Bryant for her encouragement and top-notch feedback as I completed this manuscript; Vicki Kasabian and the team at Heinemann for their flexibility and meticulous care as they produced this book.

My dad for being a prolific source of juicy math problems. My husband for listening and reflecting ideas back to me in ways that made me feel smarter. My children for getting me to play snow dinosaurs when I thought I needed to work on this book. It all adds up.

$$6+6=12 \quad 6+5=11 \quad 4+4=8 \quad 7+6=13$$
$$6-5=1 \quad 2-1=1 \quad 17-3=14 \quad 3-3=0$$
$$6\times2=12 \quad 5\times3=15 \quad 10\times2=20$$

Introduction

. . . for man and his fate must always form the chief interest of all technical endeavors. Never forget this in the midst of your diagrams and equations.

—Albert Einstein

Thirty-seven all together," my six-year-old announced, then read from her carefully handwritten page. "Fourteen chocolates. Seven chewy candies. Eleven sucky things. Four that I never saw before. And one set of plastic teeth."

On Halloween night, my daughter became a highly engaged mathematician. After counting the number of candies in all, then the number of candies in each of her established groups, she started in on some freelance multiplication: "Wait! There are two Starbursts in each packet, so I actually have eight Starbursts, not four, so that makes, eight . . . plus three . . . eleven chewy candies, not seven." She scribbled out her previous tally and moved on to figure the actual number of Smarties—those little stacks of sugar disks in cellophane—per packet and multiply (by successive addition) that number by the three packs she had collected on her trick-or-treating mission. My little princess (her costume—not my idea) was doing things with numbers I had never seen her attempt before, and none of us adults had anything to do with it. Mathematical ear candy.

How did she do it? Sheer determination. Why did she do it? She did it for love. Love of candy.

Reality is, not many of our classroom math problems—let alone our real-life math applications—are about candy. And I am not here to say that they ought to be. Rather, my point is that, when inspired, even the youngest among us is capable of dazzling and important mathematical thinking.

Yet, analyzing international comparative data, reviewing state test scores, or even talking with some math students, a researcher might draw another conclusion: that we are just not math folks here in the United States of America.

In a 2006 study, the Program for International Student Assessment (PISA) compared fifteen-year-olds in thirty industrialized nations; when it came to math, the United States ranked twenty-fourth (National Center for Education Statistics 2007). According to a January 2010, *U.S. News and World Report*, "The scores of average American high schoolers on international science and math tests continue to sink" (Clark 2010, 23). The same article cites the United States as currently ranking twenty-fourth in math, "near the bottom of the developed world." President Obama is quick to point out that in order to maintain any future competitive edge in the world marketplace, we must increase our students' achievement in math, science, engineering, and technology. "The future belongs to the nation that best educates its citizens" (quoted by Clark 2010, 27).

Meanwhile, the National Assessment of Educational Progress statistics show math scores across our nation increasing steadily over the past decade: in 2009,

33 percent of our eighth graders scored proficient or higher. In fifteen states and the District of Columbia, average scores were significantly lower: only 23 percent of California's students scored proficient, along with 19 percent of West Virginia's, and only 15 percent of Mississippi's. Our nation's frequent top scorer—Massachusetts—had 52 percent of eighth graders considered proficient in math. We applaud these achievements, yet I believe that on most grading scales, a 52 is still considered an F.

While visiting a high school classroom recently, I paused and prompted a boy whose paper had only thin blue lines where a trigonometry problem should have been. "So, what are you thinking?"

"Actually, ma'am," he looked up at me and spoke with more authority than you'd expect from a boy barely old enough to hold a driver's license. "I pretty much just coast in this class."

How many of our kids, I began to wonder, get to just coast in math class? And why do we let them?

Why Don't We *Get* Math?

In my work as a staff developer with the Denver-based Public Education & Business Coalition, I regularly visit classrooms to work with teachers and students both locally and nationally. In the schools I visit, I am consistently awed by hardworking professionals doing their level best day in and day out to implement standards-based curricula and keep up with pacing guides. Yet, over and again, I talk with devoted instructors who feel frustrated by the limited increases in their students' achievement. Why is it that, despite so much well-intended effort in classrooms, at the district level and even by our legislators, our students' progress appears stunted?

A number of systems and beliefs—cultural, educational, and individual—interfere with students' understanding of math. *yup.*

Cultural: It's Okay Not to Get It

In the introduction to the important book *Radical Equations* (Moses and Cobb 2001), Robert Moses describes our collective acceptance of low performance in math as distinct from our collective expectation that all children should and must learn to read. In my own experience as a middle school math teacher, I met with many a parent who, when confronted with a child's low achievement in math, would say something like, "Yeah, well, I never did get math either," excusing a child's low scores as reasonable—or even biologically predetermined—rather than helping me as the teacher hold up the bar.

Yet, to gain access to higher education; to make informed family decisions about finances, health, and employment; and to participate as informed citizens in our democracy, mathematical literacy is crucial. So, this social acceptance of mathematical illiteracy is a huge barrier to our children's progress and preparation for life beyond our classrooms.

Significant research points to the powerful influence teacher and parent attitudes and expectations have on student achievement, for better or for worse. We adults, therefore, have a duty not only to expect mathematical competence for our children but to model it ourselves. We can and must "get it," and, in turn, expect our children to do the same.

Pedagogical: Math Is Memorizing

Still today, in far too many classrooms, math is taught as algorithms, steps to be learned by heart and replicated under a specific set of circumstances: cross multiply and divide. Why? Often our teaching materials offer little by way of explanation.

Learners rehearse and regurgitate procedures, yet rarely understand them. This approach to math instruction strips students of their own opportunities to think creatively about mathematics, making them the couriers of ideas rather than their creators.

Although there are indeed math facts and theorems worth committing to memory, students need the gifts of time and space and coaching to construct for themselves an understanding of why a particular algorithm works.

This process builds student ownership of the content, invites learners to flex their mental muscles, and ensures that the procedure or idea being memorized actually makes sense to the student being asked to use it.

Individual: Math Ability Is Innate

In *Mindset*, researcher Dr. Carol Dweck (2006) describes two distinct belief systems: the "fixed" mindset and the "growth" mindset. According to her system, those who believe in the fixed mindset believe that ability is innate, endowed at birth; when fixed mindset people encounter difficulties, they assume them to be insurmountable. Conversely, those with the growth mindset believe that ability is the product of effort, that challenges are to be met with hard work. Math learners trapped in a fixed mindset give up when they are stuck, figuring that if they don't "get it," they never will. This is the sad story of many math learners who pass through our schools each year.

Dr. Dweck emphasizes the power of growth mindsets for all learners: researchers tracking college students found that those with a growth mindset saw an increase in their self-confidence over the course of their four years in university, while peers with fixed mindsets lost confidence. Working with star athletes, great artists, and other high achievers, Dweck came to understand that innate talent and good luck contribute very little to an individual's success. Almost consistently, she found, it is hard work and tenacity that make the difference between a champion and a chump.

Given its deciding power in a student's future, the growth mindset must be taught to all of our children and teens. We can do this by praising motivation and effort, rather than celebrating "smarts" as something intrinsic. We can encourage our students to see themselves as capable mathematicians, as well as to regard the colleagues in their community of learners as similarly competent thinkers.

Our Beliefs Shape Our Classrooms

If we believe that math is difficult or inaccessible, that the important work of math is memorizing and following procedures, and that some kids are born capable and others not, we create classrooms where teachers are experts, students are empty vessels to be filled, and failure is an acceptable option for some. We track students by abilities. We let some students entirely off the hook.

Yet, if instead we believe that all students can and must learn math, that the important work of math is thinking, and that all learners are capable of mastery, we create classrooms where teachers serve as coaches, students engage as a community of learners, and all can "get it" together. Creating such communities takes courage, effort, and patience, but the payoffs are tremendous.

All students can learn to understand and even enjoy math, including the young artist who drew this cartoon.

Minds-on Math Workshops

"Minds-on math workshop" is a phrase I coined to describe math learning experiences that require students to draw upon their intellectual resources as critical thinkers and problem solvers, rather than simply follow a given algorithm; require learners to stretch and think in new ways, rather than rehearse known skills; invite students to communicate their ideas with others, rather than secretly to the teacher; and, as a result, offer learners opportunities to attain a deeper understanding both of mathematics and of themselves as mathematicians.

Math is a community endeavor. With the support of a skilled coach, the challenge of collegial mathematicians, and the gift of time to think, all learners can and should become proficient mathematicians capable of wrestling a puzzling problem to its knees and arriving at a well-reasoned solution that they understand and can explain.

A minds-on math workshop is a learning experience in which students are challenged to grapple with their thinking and understanding about math in light of new information and challenges, to make meaning for themselves. Too often, students engage in decontextualized arithmetic, able to rely on memorized facts, whether they understand them or not. Minds-on math workshops offer students opportunities to work with what they know and to make sense for themselves in new ways.

Minds-on math workshops are rooted in a belief in all learners' abilities to succeed in math, given the requisite support. That support comes in the form of a carefully cultivated community of learners engaged in well-facilitated workshop model instruction that catalyzes students' mathematical understanding. In this model, students' learning is facilitated by classroom discourse, teacher conferring, and assessment *for* learning. By designing instruction that supports students as thinkers, creators, and problem solvers grappling with important mathematical ideas, we feed two birds with one piece of bread, preparing learners for their futures as both mathematicians and citizens of the world.

About This Book

The primary aim of this text is to describe how teachers can organize their classroom instruction as workshops that honor the primacy of student thinking, the imperative of student understanding, and the key role that classroom discourse plays in achieving both.

The book is organized into ten chapters, each with a similar structure, each written to present a new angle on the opportunities all teachers have to develop minds-on math workshops.

Each chapter begins with a problem of the day, a question for you to consider before, during, and after you read. Next, a postulate is presented, proposing how we might answer that question within the context of a minds-on math workshop. The body of each chapter presents research, classroom examples, and ideas, including a section devoted to the "yeah, buts . . ." a reader might be thinking about. Each chapter's concluding section is titled with the mathematicians' Latin refrain, "Quod Erat Demonstrandum," meaning "which was to be demonstrated."

The first five chapters of the book set the stage for a minds-on math workshop, describing what workshop is (Chapter 1), the intellectual tools math learners need (Chapter 2), the sorts of tasks that promote understanding (Chapter 3), how we can build communities of learners (Chapter 4), and the ways in which we can use discourse to promote thinking (Chapter 5). The second five chapters dissect each segment of the workshop in greater detail: opening (Chapter 6), minilessons (Chapter 7), work time (Chapter 8), conferring (Chapter 9), followed by sharing and reflection (Chapter 10).

Even as this book heads out of my hands, there is more I could say about each, more I am learning from teachers and students every day. Still, my goal in offering these chapters to you is that they can serve as a useful resource as you strive to enhance opportunities for student thinking in your math classroom. Above all, my hope is that through this text you might find new ways to inspire your students to believe that they need to, can, and will master mathematics through your minds-on math workshops.

CHAPTER 1

Minds-on Math Workshop

You cannot teach a man anything. You can only
help him find it within himself.
—*Galileo Galilei*

Problem of the Day: How can we use our time in math class to grow students' understanding?

Postulate: In minds-on math workshops, teachers apprentice young mathematicians by modeling thinking, immersing students in challenging tasks, and providing ample time for learners' creative work within a community of support.

When I was a kid, my stepfather liked to go fishing, and some Saturdays I would wake up early and go with him. I remember getting sunburned waiting and waiting for something to happen. One day, something finally did: a heavy bite on my line. I tried to reel it in but couldn't; I almost lost my grip on the rod. He stood over me, handling the fishing pole, winding the reel, fighting the fish while I kept a hold and tried to help. Once, I remember, he brushed my fingers aside so that he could wind the crank harder and faster. He landed a thirty-pound mako shark, then took a lot of photos of me standing with the fish, which was longer than I was tall. He gave me all the credit. I felt like an impostor. He had caught the fish, and we both knew it. I came to hate fishing.

I share this true story because it reminds me of how I started out as a math teacher: I held high expectations for my students, let them struggle for a bit, but promptly stepped in to rescue with explanations and answers if I saw their comprehension flagging. Far too often, and with the best of intentions, I dominated the overhead projector, vis-à-vis marker smeared on the heel of my hand, landing the proverbial fish for all to behold.

But, I soon realized, my approach was not actually helping my students to learn much math. As many continued to struggle on assessments, I sought new strategies, new means to support learners in taking ownership of their mathematical understanding.

I learned to explain less and listen more; to answer fewer questions and to ask better ones; to avoid rescuing students from confusion and instead to be patient with their uncertainty. In short, I learned to let the students do the work of thinking, which led to understanding in my math classes. That work is the work of a minds-on math workshop.

In this chapter, I offer an overview of the theory behind minds-on math workshops, as well as a vision of how they function, all of which will be fleshed out later in the book.

Purpose

Workshop model instruction is about cultivating all learners' understanding. The purpose of a minds-on math workshop is to put into practice our belief in all students' mathematical abilities by creating and facilitating learning experiences that invite individuals to construct and negotiate deep conceptual understanding, as well as develop fluency with numbers.

Rooted in social constructivism, the Deweyan notion that understanding is defined within a social unit, workshop model instruction motivates students to learn in the role of cognitive apprentice, growing understanding in conversation and collaboration with both teachers and peers. Workshop model instruction draws on Vygotsky's theory of a zone of proximal development, the notion that with the support of a community, learners can meet more strenuous challenges than they might otherwise succeed at alone (Vygotsky 1978).

Minds-on math workshops are an ideal forum for meeting the challenges laid before us by the Common Core Standards, a call, as described by James Zumba and his colleagues at Achieve the Core, for renewed focus, congruence, and rigor. Workshops offer learners time to experience

- focus: delve deeply into a concept, focus on understanding important ideas well

- congruence: make connections among big ideas that spiral from grade to grade

- rigor: balance conceptual understanding, procedural fluency, and application.

Beliefs

As a classroom teacher, I initially had a hard time limiting my mathematical theatrics. I knew my content so well, and it just made so much sense to me, and I figured I was best suited to explain everything to everyone. But it wasn't working. As I gradually adjusted my math instruction to incorporate more workshop time, I learned to smile and wait rather than answer questions, to stop creating color-coded correct answer keys on my transparencies and instead to invite students to compare their solutions. I learned to move to the side of the room and allow learners to explain their (sometimes erroneous) thinking to peers. It came down to trust: I had to trust that my students could and would master mathematics if I stopped talking at them, stopped rescuing them, and started instead giving them time to think.

As a math teacher, three important beliefs guided my evolution—beliefs that I hope you share:

- Students are capable of brilliance.

- Understanding takes time.

- There is more than one way.

Let us consider each of these in turn.

Students are capable of brilliance.

In the introduction, I described Dweck's research on fixed and growth mindsets; in her book, *Mindset*, Dr. Dweck (2006) tells the poignant story of a low achiever she called "Jimmy," who, when taught that mindset is a choice and that learners can progress through effort, looked up misty-eyed and asked, "You mean I don't have to be dumb?" (59).

Minds-on math workshops are rooted in a belief that no one needs to feel dumb and that our math learning time can be devoted to honing learners' mastery of important content by invoking, promoting, and celebrating the smart thinking of all.

Understanding takes time.

Minds-on math workshops are driven by the notion that deep and thoughtful understanding requires multiple exposures to a concept from a variety of angles and that once learners understand concepts, they become flexible problem solvers. Workshops offer students the time to attain this understanding.

As some states and districts unveil increasingly longer lists of standards and textbooks grow thicker with each edition, we need to have the courage to slow down, to adjust our goal from "coverage" to "understanding." As articulated by the Common

So am I just suppose to their peers let them fail even when help them) under stand?

Constraints: The Text, the Pacing Guide, the Assessments

Most math teachers I know work within a system of constraints that include curriculum, materials, unit plans, school schedules, department expectations, district and state tests . . . the list goes on. When they raise concerns about whether they are allowed to make changes to the way they teach and what they cover, I remind them that the goal of math instruction is student understanding. As long as teachers continue to target the learning goals agreed upon by their department, district, or curriculum and students can demonstrate understanding on the periodic standardized assessments, administrators tend to be flexible with teachers exploring new means to those ends.

As you continue reading this chapter, remember that minds-on math workshops target student understanding, not curriculum coverage, though those objectives are not mutually exclusive. Coming to understand linear equations may not necessarily have to entail every student graphing all thirty equations presented on page 108 of the textbook: Students' learning activities could look different, but understanding linear equations remains the goal.

Core Standards for Mathematics, process skills—referred to there as "mathematical practices"—are transferrable to all strands of mathematics at all levels; minds-on math workshops are an ideal place to cultivate students' agility with these practices with repeated exposure to each.

On the importance of learning with understanding, math professor James Hiebert explains, "If we want students to know what mathematics is, as a subject, they must understand it. Knowing mathematics, really knowing it, means understanding it. When we memorize rules for moving symbols around on paper, we may be learning something, but we are not learning mathematics" (1997, 2).

There is more than one way.

Though there is often only one correct *answer* to a mathematical question, there may be an infinite variety of ways to arrive at that answer, to think about and understand its meaning. Rather than devoting time to memorizing algorithms (cross multiply and divide), minds-on math workshops invite students to employ math practices and approaches that work for them. Minds-on math workshops open doors to creative thinking and unique problem-solving methodologies, target conceptual understanding, and promote intellectual flexibility.

With faith that each child, given time, has an innate ability to reason out a solution to a problem, even if their initial approach and strategy may differ from how we believe things "ought" to be done, we can begin to turn over the responsibility for learning mathematics to our students. This alone can be a challenge: Giving students control of the conversation can feel unsettling to a teacher who has spent time earnestly trying to stave off confusion. Yet, to learn best, students need to be fully engaged as thinkers, rather than permitted to sit passively while we perform mathematical stunts.

This is not to say we should toss each student a prealgebra book and then go check our email; rather, I propose a carefully structured learning environment and specific use of time that invites math learners to purposefully engage as a community in worthy tasks designed to draw forth their understanding.

I do this

Workshops' History

Many celebrated literacy instructors have honed readers' and writers' workshops: Lucy Calkins, Nancie Atwell, Cynthia Greenleaf, and Samantha Bennett, among others. Describing her own shift in developing workshop model instruction, Atwell explains that she needed to "stop focusing on myself and my curriculum and start observing my students" (1998, 4). Minds-on math workshops stand on the shoulders of these literacy teachers and their proven ideas about effective instruction.

When it comes to math workshops, Catherine Fosnot and her colleagues have developed wonderful resources for the elementary level, and curricula such as the Connected Math Program draw on the notion of workshop model instruction. The purpose of this book is to clarify how teachers can create and sustain math workshops that retain a focus on student experiences and student thinking and that culminate in deep understanding—*minds-on* math workshops.

Workshop model instruction is essentially a modern incarnation of a classic strategy: apprenticing learners alongside a master craftsperson. As Samantha Bennett describes, "The basic paradigm shift—flipping the definition of teaching as talking to teaching as listening and allocating classroom time accordingly—sits at the core of the structural shift in the use of time in a workshop. When workshop works, the bulk of classroom time is dedicated to students reading, writing and talking, not listening to someone else talk" (2007, 12).

The purpose, then, of a minds-on math workshop is for students to build confidence and competence as members of a community of mathematicians. To this end, learners in a well-designed workshop will

- engage with worthy, minds-on tasks and important mathematical ideas
- enjoy time to think, work, and communicate
- construct mathematical understanding for themselves, and
- notice their own development as mathematicians.

The context of a workshop provides for all of these, as the teacher's role changes from that of presenter to that of facilitator.

The workshop model is based on the principle that in each class, students devote the majority of their time to thinking and talking about important mathematical ideas because those doing the most work are doing the most learning.

Key Aspects of Workshops

Four key aspects of a minds-on math workshop bring learning to life:

- challenging tasks
- community
- collaboration and discourse
- conferring.

In the next section of this chapter, we will explore each of these aspects of a successful workshop to gain a broad overview. The remainder of the text will delve more deeply into the structure where we put these key elements to work.

Challenging Tasks: Minds On

For many years, math and science teachers have sought to introduce "hands-on" activities, which can be highly engaging and, at times, intellectually challenging. Better than simply offering kinesthetic experiences, we need to ensure that all tasks are *minds-on*, that is, requiring students to immerse themselves in challenging thinking that culminates in conceptual understanding.

In order for students to devote their time in math class to reasoning and communicating as thoughtful mathematicians, we need to offer them something worthy to chew on with their intellectual teeth. A rich math workshop is centered around minds-on tasks that require deep thinking and evoke understanding. In Chapter 3, we will look more closely at the attributes of high-quality minds-on tasks.

Community

If you are starting to wonder how one might facilitate academic discourse or confer with learners during a chapter of *Lord of the Flies*, you are thinking about the requisite groundwork that both of these sorts of interaction require: community. And not just any old community, but a learning-focused culture where students value intellectual honesty, respect their peers' ideas and needs, and are more keen to understand concepts than to "be right" (Ritchhart 2002).

Community is a tangible feeling one can experience when entering the classroom of a master teacher; it is created on so many levels: by the physical layout of the room, the structure of the learning tasks, the conversations between folks, the systems for reinforcing expectations. The interactions of a minds-on math workshop require the groundwork of a strong community, one where all students feel safe to risk sharing their thinking, so Chapter 4 is devoted to uncovering community's key ingredients.

Collaboration and Discourse

Students' ability to engage collaboratively in classroom discourse—have engaged, accountable (Resnick 2006) conversations about their learning—is critical to the success of the workshop model. Discourse promotes thinking, builds community, and invites metacognition. Discourse is a life skill, and math classes are wonderful learning grounds for the listening, critical thinking, and cooperation that discourse requires.

Some teachers I have worked with hesitate to invite student collaboration or classroom discussion out of concern that students may be either unprepared or incapable of learning in these ways: "They just can't work together." "They don't know how to explain their thinking." "They only listen when I am talking." "They will get us off track, and we have to stay on pace." All of these statements may well be true in those particular classrooms. Yet, collaboration and discourse are learned skills, ones that instructors can model, explain, practice, and assess just as we would any other skill. Time devoted to cultivating classroom discourse supports students not only in their math learning, but also in developing life skills that will serve them long after they leave our classrooms. Collaboration and discourse will be explored in greater detail in Chapter 5.

Conferring

Related to yet distinct from collaboration, *conferring* describes a particular sort of discourse that takes place between a teacher and student focused together around understanding a concept. Teachers confer by sitting with individuals or small groups of learners, listening in to what they may be thinking and wondering, then offering a targeted nudge toward deeper mathematical understanding. In the context of math workshop, teachers seize opportunities provided by the work time to confer with students in order to instruct and assess. Conferring is described more fully in Chapter 9.

Structure of a Workshop

What makes workshop model instruction unique and distinct from typical classroom instruction is the focus on student thinking before, during, and after work time.

In a minds-on math workshop, a minilesson is devoted to apprenticing students in the kinds of *thinking* required to complete a task, rather than offering a procedure to

* I do a terrible job with reflection.

follow. During work time, students may identify a range of strategies that could bring them to accurate solutions. Then, during the reflection, students are asked to consider the ideas and solutions of peers and reflect on their own evolving understanding.

Recalling the concept of apprenticeship described previously, we can envision our math workshop as an opportunity to briefly teach, then invite students to wrestle with ideas, then reflect on how their thinking has grown and changed through this experience. As articulated by literacy instructors, a workshop divides the class period into distinct segments, known commonly as the opening, the minilesson, work time, and reflection (Bennett 2007).

This use of time provides for direct instruction, small-group or independent work, followed by opportunities for metacognition, a chance for individuals to step outside of themselves and notice their own thoughts, growth, and questions.

Many teachers' instruction approximates workshop model: some initial explanation followed by work time. Yet, minds-on math workshops differ in some important ways. Let's take just a quick look at each segment.

The chart below begins to introduce the nuances of each segment in a minds-on math workshop; throughout this chapter, we will explore those in greater detail.

If a workshop model lesson were a pizza cut into sixteen equal pieces, the first two slices would be the opening, the next three the minilesson, the next eight work time, and the remaining slices would be reserved for sharing and reflection, though these proportions can be adjusted, as we will discuss later. (See Figure 1.1.)

In this chapter, I will offer a general overview of each component of the workshop, as well as share some illustrative excerpts of a transcript from Rachel Rosenberg

	Typical Approximation	**Minds-on Math Workshop**
Opening	Students do a problem designed to get them seated and quiet while teacher takes attendance.	Learners work on a problem designed to draw out their prior knowledge related to the day's learning goal(s).
Minilesson	Teacher gives instructions and shows students how to do their work.	Teacher states the purpose for their work, models thinking, welcomes multiple strategies.
Work Time	Students work on problem sets while teacher helps.	Students engage with challenging tasks while teacher confers.
Reflection	Teacher verifies that students "get it."	Students discuss what they understand about the concept and how their thinking as mathematicians has changed.

Figure 1.1 *Who's doing the work?*

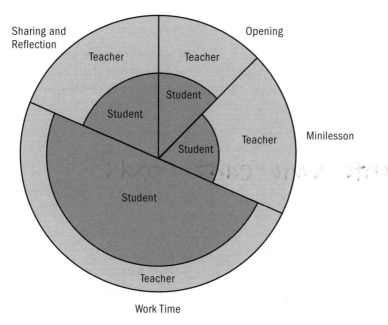

and her fourth graders at Denver's Harrington Elementary School. A master teacher who has honed her ability to facilitate students' deep mathematical understanding, Rachel graciously opens her doors several times a year to educators from across the country who come as lab visitors. She and the other teachers I will introduce in this book are exemplars of the practices integral to minds-on math workshops; listening in on them and their students at work will help paint the picture of what the practices described here look like in reality. During the lesson included here, Rachel and her students were beginning to explore the challenge of adding fractions.

Opening

In many effective math classrooms, students start class with an independent task that invites them to draw upon their prior understanding and begin to wrestle with the content of the day. Teachers call these "warm-ups," "problems of the day," "day starters," or various other names. Regardless of the name one may choose, the purpose behind these opening problems is to engage students as thinkers in the work of that day's lesson and springboard them into high-quality discourse about the mathematical concept.

Let's listen in as Rachel invites students to get started on a problem that draws out their background knowledge about adding fractions, offering her a perfect launch pad from which to delve into her minilesson.

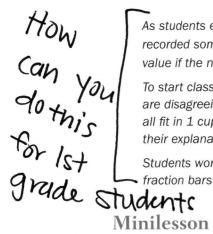

How can you do this for 1st grade students who can't read?

> As students enter the classroom, they see a chart where Rachel has recorded some of their questions about fractions: What happens to the value if the numerators are different? Can fractions be even or odd?
>
> To start class, Rachel hands out a word problem: "Bessie and her friend are disagreeing about whether ½ cup of coffee and ²/₆ cup of milk will all fit in 1 cup." She asks the students not only for an answer but also for their explanation.
>
> Students work silently for about five minutes. Some write, draw, or get fraction bars and click them around.

Minilesson

Using the opening as a springboard, teachers then dive into a minilesson designed to orient students to the purpose of the day's work, then introduce or revisit concepts and strategies that will be useful during independent work time. This whole-group instruction can be done in the form of a think-aloud demonstration or shared practice on a problem parallel to one that students will tackle later.

Notice in the excerpt that follows that the focus of Rachel's minilesson is problem solving, then she closes with instructions and expectations for the day's work time.

> After students have had time to work on the opening, Rachel explains their purpose: to deepen their understanding about addition with fractions. She puts the problem up on a document camera. She models the process she would go through to solve the problem, "thinking aloud" as she goes. She demonstrates how she would read the problem once for the general gist, then again to identify and underline important information. She draws a picture to model the problem, finds an answer, checks it for reasonableness, then redoes the calculation when she determines that her answer was not reasonable—all steps she wants the students to use in solving a problem.
>
> Rachel then asks students to talk with a partner about what they noticed during her modeling, and which strategies they might use later to solve problems requiring the addition of fractions. After a few minutes of discussion, they share an abundance of ideas, drawing on their observation of Rachel as well as their own experience: draw a picture, write the numbers, use multiples to find a common denominator, try fraction bars, think whether the answer is reasonable, use a measuring cup and fill it, don't give up. Though Rachel does demonstrate her own problem solving, she

then invites students to name for themselves and their peers a menu of the kinds of thinking they could use to solve similar problems.

After this discussion, Rachel challenges students with a new, related problem: "Bessie convinced José that $^2/_6 + ^1/_3 = ^3/_9$. Do you agree?" She requests five minutes of silence as the students begin work.

Work Time

The bulk of a minds-on math workshop is devoted to work time. This time can be structured in a variety of ways, but often begins with students sinking their teeth into a juicy problem either individually or in small groups. Rather than zipping through a problem set containing numerous calculations to complete or equations to solve, learners may devote this work time to wrestling with one or two meaty problems that both catalyze and require conceptual understanding and invite students to carefully articulate and document their thinking. Teachers then use work time as an opportunity to differentiate instruction by offering a range of challenge levels in a task, a variety of support, and an array of tools for students to use. Work time also works best when students have additional mathematical responsibilities to attend to in the event that they are "done" with the work of the day.

Often during this work time, teachers will "catch and release" learners (Bennett 2007). This involves pressing a pause button of sorts on the work time to call the group's attention back together to answer important questions, invite students to share thinking, or clarify expectations.

Work time is also a key opportunity for a teacher to confer with learners about their mathematical thinking. Distinct from the traditional "helping" I used to do (which often meant I would grab a stuck kid's pencil and do the next two steps of the algebra problem for her), conferring is a chance for a teacher to listen and understand what and how students are thinking about their own problem solving, nudge them along, and encourage independence. Let's peek back into Rachel's class to see what might happen during a work time.

As students begin working on whether $^2/_6 + ^1/_3 = ^3/_9$, some fetch manipulatives to use at their tables, others begin with graph paper, and others grab markers. Rachel chooses one student and kneels down next to him. In a whisper, she talks with him about the problem. "So, what are you thinking? . . . Why?" She listens as he explains his thinking. Then she moves on to confer with another student.

After five minutes, Rachel rings a bell to get students' attention. She asks how things are going, and whether students have any questions. They clarify some points: Which one is the denominator? Can they use fraction bars? Rachel answers their questions, and encourages those who finish to attend to their other responsibilities. She reminds learners to document their work with "Be ready to share your thinking on the rug."

As students turn back to their fractions, Rachel calls a small group to meet with her. These are all the students she noticed were struggling during the first few minutes of work time. She inquires about their various methods so far and asks what they are noticing about the problem:

- *"These fractions are listed smallest to greatest."*

- *"You can't add the denominators if they are not alike."*

- *"Are we comparing fractions?" (This is what they had been doing the previous week, which this learner is still thinking about.)*

- *"The answer has to be bigger than $2/6$."*

Rachel asks students how they can use their tools to solve the problem. They offer various methods—drawing, fraction bars, finding common denominators. She asks more questions: "Is $2/6$ greater or less than $1/2$? Is $1/3$ closer to a whole, or closer to 0?" When she turns the students back to work, they use fraction bars and draw sketches as they puzzle over her questions.

Other groups are talking quietly at their tables, using manipulatives, solving the problem, and recording their thinking in words, numbers, and pictures. As they finish, they get out other math material to work on—a routine Rachel had established early in the year.

Sharing and Reflection

Tempting as it may be to allow learners to work right up to the bell, astute practitioners of workshop model instruction value and prioritize time for sharing and reflection at the close of each workshop. At this time, students come back together as a whole group to talk about solutions or challenges, what they do and do not yet understand, or how they are now thinking about themselves as mathematicians. Reflection can be oral, as well as in writing, and offers responsive teachers an opportunity to know where students stand in order to plan the next day's instruction accordingly.

Rachel calls students back together, inviting them to bring "your questions, your thinking, and your clickers." The students sit in a circle with their math work in their laps. Rachel asks Hannah to share.

Challenging tasks	Rather than asking students to simply complete a series of fraction addition problems using a known algorithm, Rachel asked them to think deeply about one particular problem and used it to leverage their understanding of what numerators and denominators actually represent.
Collaboration/ discourse	Rather than asking students to either work alone or work in groups, Rachel fostered discourse by asking each learner to start problem solving independently before entering into a conversation with his or her group, ensuring each student had some initial thinking to bring to the table.
Community	Rather than playing the role of reigning expert in the room, Rachel invited students to share their thinking and to reflect on the thinking at regular intervals throughout the class.
Conferring	Rather than retreating to administrative tasks while the students worked, Rachel seized this opportunity to get down at eye level with learners and inquire about their thinking and understanding.

"I really didn't get it so I asked for help."

"What didn't you get? What was confusing to you?"

"I added $2/6 + 1/3$, and I also came up with $3/9$."

Rachel asks, "What did you say to yourself?"

"It's not reasonable."

"Why not?"

Hannah points to her work, now projected on the screen from the document camera.

"What does she need?" Rachel asks the group.

One student offers, "She needs to remember that you don't add the denominator."

"Why?" Rachel probes. "We can't just say because you can't add denominators. We want to understand why. Why can't you do that?" Students discuss the question with a partner, and then share their ideas with the group.

"How has your thinking changed today as a mathematician?" Rachel invites, and students turn and talk some more.

Finally, Rachel puts up one last problem: $2/4 + 1/8 = 3/12$. "Is this true or false? Turn and talk to a partner about what you are going to answer and *why. Then use your clicker to answer." After the discussion, Rachel posts a graph of the students' responses.*

Throughout this brief visit to Rachel's classroom, we can see the interplay of the four elements described earlier: challenging tasks; collaboration and discourse; community; and conferring.

Though 98 percent of Rachel's students qualify for free and reduced lunch and 76 percent are English language learners, they consistently outperform state and district peers on standardized measures of student achievement: in 2008, although only 48 percent of Denver Public Schools' fourth graders scored proficient or advanced on our state mathematics test, 60 percent of Rachel's students did so. Teachers who embrace workshop model mathematics instruction find that not only are their students more engaged, but they also make significant gains in achievement.

Outcomes

A hardware store near our house offers Saturday morning workshops: for a few dollars, a parent and child can receive instruction and all the materials they need to build bookends, a step stool, a birdhouse, whatever the project is that month. A kid participating in one of these sessions goes home delighted with their creation, but the parents likely realize the outcomes of the workshop extend far beyond the birdhouse they need to install on their porch: skills with hand tools, an appreciation for how things are made, and a strengthened parent-child relationship, to name a few.

Similarly, the outcomes of a minds-on math workshop stretch far beyond the problems completed or even the test scores students achieve. The deeper objective of a math workshop is developing student's conceptual understanding of mathematics. Related outcomes include student agency, confidence, and twenty-first-century skills: problem solving, collaboration, critical thinking, and communication.

"Yeah, but . . ."

"How can you spend all that time on just one problem? Don't kids need practice?"

Minds-on math workshops prioritize time for students to construct meaning, rather than memorize and rehearse algorithms. Digging into one significant problem that requires deep conceptual understanding can be a worthy investment. As you saw in Rachel's class, students really

WHO DOES WHAT WHEN IN A MINDS-ON MATH WORKSHOP?

	Teacher	Student
Opening	◆ Welcomes learners ◆ Sets purpose ◆ Challenges students to start thinking	◆ Settles into class ◆ Starts thinking by solving a problem or responding to a prompt
Minilesson	◆ Activates background knowledge ◆ Models thinking ◆ Demonstrates use of tools ◆ Models math content ◆ Sets expectations for work time	◆ Listens, watches, takes notes ◆ Asks clarifying questions ◆ Practices thinking alongside teacher
Work Time	◆ Confers with students ◆ Supports small groups as needed ◆ Assesses students' understanding	◆ Applies learning from minilesson to math learning experience ◆ Engages in mathematical problem solving ◆ Collaborates with peers in ways that promote thinking and understanding ◆ Documents thinking
Sharing and Reflection	◆ Facilitates students' sharing ◆ Connects students' learning to larger purpose of the lesson ◆ Acknowledges students' progress and effort ◆ Describes next steps in the learning sequence	◆ Shares thinking ◆ Asks questions ◆ Synthesizes ◆ Monitors how thinking has grown or changed

had to wrestle with the significance of the denominator to be able to approach the problem successfully. This understanding is foundational to their future work on operations with fractions. Once students grasp the concept, practice will be more efficient because the big idea is already solidified. Devoting time to a well-chosen problem, students can dive in, make sense, allay misconceptions, and articulate their thinking in ways that a more typical problem set may not invite.

"During all that work time, what if students get completely off base?"

When visitors observe an effective workshop model classroom, they are often stunned by the ways in which the "classroom runs itself." Students can achieve an amazing level of self-sufficiency with great effort, targeted scaffolding, and teacher vigilance. Crucial ingredients for a focused workshop include clear minilessons, frequent monitoring, and redirection through the "catch and release" process, collaboration and peer support, differentiation through conferring, and work with invitational small groups.

Still, students can lose their way. Astute teachers channel misconceptions as teachable moments; confusion can be great fodder for learning. These side trips can uncover significant, common errors that a savvy teacher can use to propel the whole class toward deeper knowledge. Sometimes it's messy, yet the product—student understanding—is well worth the struggle.

Quod Erat Demonstrandum

Minds-on math workshops are complex. They are designed and facilitated to apprentice all students in the work of mathematical thinking and to create opportunities for each to land the sharks of conceptual understanding by themselves.

Minds-on math workshops require challenging tasks, collaboration, community, and conferring within the context of a specific organization of time that maximizes opportunities for student thinking. If you share the belief that all students are capable of brilliance, that our responsibility as teachers is to foster their thinking, then you need not fret that you might do this "wrong." If your students are wrestling with ideas, sharing their thoughts, and making progress as mathematicians, you are on the right track. The pages ahead are laid out to help expedite your journey—and theirs.

WORKSHOP PLANNING TEMPLATE

	Teacher	Student
Opening		
Minilesson		
Work Time		
Sharing and Reflection		

CHAPTER 2

Tools

My view is that we should describe the skills that students will be expected to master—rather than just the content they will memorize—in every discipline, for every grade level. In the 21st century, where information is constantly changing and readily available on any PC, competencies matter far more than content coverage.

—*Tony Wagner*

Problem of the Day: How do you teach students to understand information and solve problems for themselves?

Postulate: The purpose of minds-on math workshops is twofold: to support students in understanding math concepts and simultaneously to develop students' mastery of transferable skills and strategies that will help them to succeed across content areas, throughout the stages of their lives.

What do you do when you are reading and get hung up on a word?" I asked one young learner.

"Oh, I sound it out, or I chunk it, or I look inside it and see if I recognize any parts, or I start back at the beginning of the sentence and get a running start and see if I can figure out what word would make sense."

"You have a lot of strategies. Where did you learn those?"

"School. First grade."

"What about in math? What do you do when you get stuck?"

"I don't know. I start over. But it's really hard because if I did it wrong the first time, how am I supposed to try it again and get it right?"

This learner was attending a school where math teachers often complained that students did not know how to think and argued that thinking was not something they could teach.

We *can* teach students to think, and we must. Just as this learner acquired skills and strategies for approaching unknown words, she can also be taught how to attack troubling math problems, how to think her way through confusion. Honing these skills is the work of a minds-on math workshop. Every student ought to know that getting stuck is part of learning math and to have in her tool belt a collection of possible options to employ—independently and flexibly—when the inevitable occurs.

We can embed the teaching of these transferable approaches—practices, skills, strategies—in content-rich learning experiences, as promoted in the Common Core standards. Teaching thinking of this sort takes time; workshop model instruction affords us that time, time to describe, model, practice, and reflect upon the efficacy of each new tool offered.

Learners in minds-on math workshop can describe with confidence their strategies for allaying confusion: "When I get stuck, I try to think of it in another way. I go back to my purpose and figure out what is important, what details I have missed, or if I have more background knowledge about the problem. I think about how I could model the situation with a table or a picture or something, and I ask other kids to explain how they are thinking about it. Then I usually can get into it." What if all of our students could say this about how they get "unstuck"?

As Dr. Dweck (2006) describes, learning and growth are the fruit of hard work and effort. Yet, if students do not grasp *how* to do the work—the thinking—of mathematicians, they do not know how to try harder. They are trapped going back and repeating their mistakes, perhaps in better penmanship. Our role as growth-minded teachers is to reveal to students what goes on inside the black box of a mathematician's mind, apprenticing them to our own thinking, introducing learners to an array of strategies they can adopt and adapt to become problem solvers in their own right.

"As in reading," writes Maggie Siena, "comprehension is the ultimate goal of mathematics. And as in reading, teachers can no longer rest on the assumption that when a mathematical skill is mastered, understanding will naturally follow. Instead, we need to teach students what math comprehension means—what it feels like to really understand the math they do—and how they can develop it" (2009, 34).

In this chapter, we will explore some tools that not only build student agency in math but also equip students to grapple with greater intellectual challenges in the years to come:

- Common Core mathematical practices
- twenty-first-century skills
- thinking strategies.

In addition, I will describe how teachers can integrate instruction and experience with these tools into content-focused math workshops. But first, let us start with our purpose: understanding.

Constructing Understanding

What if all students routinely experienced intellectually engaging and challenging learning lives? What if they were taught that ideas worth understanding are worth the struggle? What if teachers modeled the power of struggle so that students wouldn't fear, but embrace difficulty and challenge?

—**Ellin Oliver Keene, To Understand**

Every school, district, and state I have visited provides teachers with clear standards—the *what*—of their math instruction: the stuff we want the kids to understand. As ever-increasing amounts of information are available with the click of a button and the landscape of learning morphs to catch up with evolving technology, students, more than ever, need to know *how* to learn, rather than *what* to know. As Einstein (2002) himself famously exhorted, "Never memorize something you can look up."

So right there alongside that *what*, we need to teach the *how*: how to think and construct understanding for one's self. We cannot ask students to dig without shovels or fly without wings. Learners deserve to be taught strategies for moving from confusion to comprehension all on their own.

What is the comprehension, this understanding we are after? For the purpose of this conversation, I offer a simple working definition of *understanding*: the construction of meaning, meaning that can be remembered and reapplied in new situations. Chapter 3 delves further into this notion of understanding and the design of tasks to that end. Here, though, it is simply important to agree on two principles:

- Mathematical understanding is a key outcome of math learning experiences.
- Teaching students the means to attain that understanding is our critical role as math instructors.

Understanding is hard work. It requires time, effort, skill, and patience, some of which may not come naturally to the learners in our charge. We must, then, model each of these, support students in strengthening their endurance, embracing a growth mindset, and gathering into their tool belts the skills they will need to build their own understanding.

Tools of the Trade

Recently, researchers and educational theorists, conscious of the quantum changes afoot in our society, have stepped back and looked at what students really need to succeed as mathematicians, as well as citizens. Authors of the Common Core provide us with a broad list of mathematical practices (some adapted from previous National Council of Teachers of Mathematics standards) that support students' success as math learners at every level. Proponents of twenty-first-century skills, in examining the demands of the workplace, developed a list of skills we can explicitly teach learners in order to prepare them to thrive in a variety of settings. Additionally, research on proficient readers brings us a list of strategies useful to learners across content areas as they wrestle with information and ideas.

These lists offer us a smorgasbord of options. As teachers, we can look at the content and tasks we are introducing; decide which tools—practices, skills, and strategies—are best suited to supporting learners; and then explicitly offer instruction on these processes within the context of content learning. In this way, we capitalize on math learning experiences as opportunities to introduce and reinforce transferable competencies.

The Common Core Standards of Mathematical Practice

Wisely, authors of the 2010 Common Core documents clarified specific grade-level learning objectives by strand of mathematics, then overlaid on top of these a set of practices that all students ought to be exposed to at every of grade level as they proceed with their math studies:

Standards of Mathematical Practice from the Common Core State Standards

1. Make sense of problems and persevere in solving them.
2. Reason abstractly and quantitatively.
3. Construct viable arguments and critique the reasoning of others.
4. Model with mathematics.
5. Use appropriate tools strategically.
6. Attend to precision.
7. Look for and make use of structure.
8. Look for and express regularity in repeated reasoning.

INTEGRATING STANDARDS OF MATHEMATICAL PRACTICE
INTO MINDS-ON MATH WORKSHOPS

	Minilesson	Work Time	Sharing and Reflection
1. Make sense of problems and persevere in solving them.	◆ Explicitly teach strategies for dissecting text, representing problems, and solving them. ◆ Discuss and intentionally build students' endurance.	◆ Scaffold students' independence. ◆ Offer ample time to explore a variety of solutions. ◆ Recognize and encourage stamina.	◆ Welcome many approaches to problem solving. ◆ Reflect upon the efficacy of specific strategies. ◆ Celebrate perseverance.
2. Reason abstractly and quantitatively.	◆ Teach math as reasoning and sense making. ◆ Model logical reasoning. ◆ Teach students to support claims with evidence.	◆ Invite learners to solve problems using methods that make sense to them. ◆ Create opportunities for discourse about methods.	◆ Ask learners to explain their logic, how they arrived at solutions.
3. Construct viable arguments and critique the reasoning of others.	◆ Teach learners how to express their ideas and thinking. ◆ Teach learners to respond respectfully to the thinking of peers.	◆ Promote a respectful community of learners. ◆ Maintain a safe climate for sharing thinking.	◆ Have learners present their solutions and the thinking behind them to peers. ◆ Encourage respectful discussion of learners' ideas.
4. Model with mathematics.	◆ Introduce a variety of mental models. ◆ Demonstrate how to transfer information from one representation to another.	◆ Offer learners opportunities to make meaning of a variety of models. ◆ Encourage learners to create models that they themselves find meaningful.	◆ Reflect on the value of a range of models given a particular purpose.

5. Use appropriate tools strategically.	◆ Introduce a variety of tools. ◆ Teach learners appropriate use of tools. ◆ Teach learners to care for tools.	◆ Make all tools accessible to students throughout work time. ◆ Offer tasks that invite use of a variety of tools.	◆ Invite learners to consider how helpful specific tools were or were not for a given task.
6. Attend to precision.	◆ Model precision. ◆ Demonstrate techniques that ensure precision. ◆ Value accuracy over speed.	◆ Allow ample work time. ◆ Encourage peers to attend to precision throughout work time. ◆ Pause to invite self-monitoring.	◆ Reflect on factors that promote or detract from precision. ◆ Strategize around common errors and the means to avoid those.
7. Look for and make use of structure.	◆ Model how to find patterns. ◆ Discuss how identifying patterns and structures can assist mathematicians in understanding information.	◆ Challenge learners to use structure and patterns to help them solve problems. ◆ Practice decomposing numbers, equations, and expressions into their composite parts.	◆ Explore how students made sense of numbers and problems by considering structure and patterns. ◆ Discuss how structure and patterns helped learners solve problems.
8. Look for and express regularity in repeated reasoning.	◆ Explore how repeated reasoning can help mathematicians make sense of situations and solve problems. ◆ Demonstrate how equations, graphs, and other mathematical representations summarize patterns.	◆ Offer in-depth tasks that invite learners to monitor the reasonableness of solutions. ◆ Invite learners to generalize from patterns and to express those generalizations mathematically. ◆ Use regularity to monitor for accuracy.	◆ Share how learners as mathematicians expressed regularity. ◆ Discuss how monitoring for regularity helped students check their solutions. ◆ Reflect on how repeated reasoning helps learners solve problems.

If all of our students were capable of each of these, they would be well on their way as independent problem solvers! To support learners in attaining that level of mastery, we need to not only refer to these practices but unpack them, break down each, and clarify what they are and how we practice them.

Middle school math teacher Deb Maruyama is a shining example of teaching students to "Make sense of problems and persevere in solving them." She devotes class time and conversation to the notion of getting "stuck and unstuck," honoring that this is a process all mathematicians experience and providing students with an array of strategies to use to "unstick" themselves. When her students struggle to solve problems, they talk about being stuck, they talk about why they are stuck, what they tried, and how that worked to get them unstuck. In this way, Deb has brought the vague notion of perseverance down to a practical level for her eighth graders.

We can utilize the structure of workshop to enhance students' abilities to embrace all eight of these practices promoted in the Common Core document. Let us consider opportunities to integrate each of these practices at each stage of our minds-on math workshops, many of which will be explored in greater detail in this chapter and others.

While it would be impractical to envision ourselves highlighting each of these practices at each stage of our workshop every day, this table (pp. 22–23) can serve as a menu of options for us as we consider ways to make explicit our instruction around the Common Core Standards of Mathematical Practice. More details on each of these practices can be found on the Common Core website. Later in this chapter, we will explore the ways in which the comprehension strategies offer specific avenues to guide students in the practices detailed here, especially the first four.

Twenty-First-Century Skills

Based on research by Dr. Tony Wagner, the Partnership for 21st Century Skills makes a call to action: We need to reinvent our educational systems to better prepare students for future realities:

> In an economy driven by innovation and knowledge . . . in marketplaces engaged in intense competition and constant renewal . . . in a world of tremendous opportunities and risks . . . in a society facing complex business, political, scientific, technological, health and environmental challenges . . . and in diverse workplaces and communities that hinge on collaborative relationships and social networking . . . the ingenuity, agility and skills of the American people are crucial to U.S. competitiveness."
> (Partnership for 21st Century Schools 2008)

INTEGRATING TWENTY-FIRST-CENTURY SKILLS INTO MINDS-ON MATH WORKSHOPS

	Minilesson	Work Time	Sharing and Reflection
Creativity and innovation	♦ Welcome divergent thinking. ♦ Model a variety of approaches.	♦ Ask open-ended questions. ♦ Invite learners to engage in ambiguous tasks. ♦ Invite learners to show thinking in myriad formats.	♦ Notice and name intentional innovation. ♦ Celebrate thinking behind all methods.
Critical thinking and problem solving	♦ Teach thinking strategies to support learners in successfully approaching puzzling problems.	♦ Offer challenging, multifaceted tasks. ♦ Create a community of learners where it is safe to risk thinking.	♦ Invite learners to critique thinking of peers. ♦ Encourage reflection on efficacy of various methods.
Communication and collaboration	♦ Teach students to think and talk as mathematicians. ♦ Explicitly teach students to document their thinking in writing. ♦ Scaffold the skills of successful collaborative learning experiences.	♦ Use structures that promote discourse. ♦ Work and learn in pairs and small groups. ♦ Create multiple opportunities for learners to articulate and explain their thinking, orally and in writing.	♦ Invite learners to think and talk about how well their team worked together. ♦ Invite learners to reflect on efficacy of collaboration in supporting student understanding.

These learning and innovation skills are deemed central to students' success not only in school but also as members of their communities and of the increasingly global workforce:

- creativity and innovation
- critical thinking and problem solving
- communication and collaboration.

Looking at this list, we can feel fortunate to teach math, where we have abundant room to hone all of them. The context of a minds-on math workshop offers explicit opportunities to practice each.

During a minilesson, we offer learners skills and strategies for innovation and creativity, demonstrating and discussing an array of possible approaches; in work time, students apply their learning from the minilesson and delve into critical thinking and problem solving, often in collaboration with others. Our learning communities thrive on communication and collaboration. In the table on page 25, we take a closer look into a workshop and consider opportunities to integrate each.

In later chapters of this book, I highlight the ways in which twenty-first-century skills can be naturally infused into the work of workshops.

Just as with any other skill, twenty-first-century skills need not only to be experienced but also to be explained, described, and reflected upon, as will be discussed later in this chapter.

Thinking Strategies

Some of the Common Core Standards of Mathematical Practice and twenty-first-century skills are so expansive that they can be challenging to pin down and explicitly teach. The thinking strategies provide us with distinct and specific avenues to guide students toward the practices and skills described above.

Thinking strategies spawned from the body of proficient reader research synthesized by David Pearson and colleagues in the early 1980s. They asked the question: What do successful readers do to make sense of new information? Seven distinct strategies emerged:

- asking questions
- determining importance
- drawing on background knowledge
- inferring
- making mental models
- monitoring for meaning
- synthesizing.

Soon after Pearson's research surfaced, Ellin Keene, Cris Tovani, and other savvy educators took these strategies into classrooms, figuring that if these were the tools proficient readers use automatically, then we ought to go ahead and teach those same approaches to all learners to increase their effectiveness as readers. Over time, educators observed the value of these strategies across the curriculum for students wrestling to make meaning of new ideas in all content areas.

THINKING STRATEGIES IN MATH

Strategy	Definition	Students say . . .	Teachers ask . . .
Asking questions	Inquire about the nature of a concept or problem in order to deepen understanding.	"What I am wondering is . . ." "How? Why? What?"	"What questions do you have?" "What are you wondering?"
Determining importance	Given a specific purpose, seek relevant and significant data or information.	"This is important." "I need to know . . ." "What I need to find out is . . ."	"What's important?" "What's the big idea here?" "What are you being asked to do?"
Drawing on background knowledge	Use what's already known to make sense of new information.	"I remember . . ." "This is like . . ."	"What does this remind you of?" "What do you already know about . . . ?" "What kind of math are you being asked to do?"
Inferring	Draw conclusions based on information given.	"I think what I am supposed to do is . . . because . . ." "I'm guessing that . . . because . . ."	"What are you thinking?" "What do you think this is all about?"
Making mental models	Represent ideas and information in multiple formats.	"I am picturing . . ." (drawing graphs, sketches, diagrams, or other representations)	"How could you represent this situation?" "What kinds of mental models might you make?"
Monitoring for meaning	Be aware of when one does and does not understand, and use fix-up strategies accordingly.	"I'm confused . . ." "So, what I understand is . . ." "Wait, this doesn't make sense."	"What do you understand?" "What part makes sense?" "Do you agree with yourself?"
Synthesizing	Grow thinking over time.	"Oh! Now I understand." "First I thought . . . but now I am thinking . . ."	"How have your ideas changed?" "What have you learned about yourself as a mathematician here?"

Figure 2.1 *Background Knowledge*

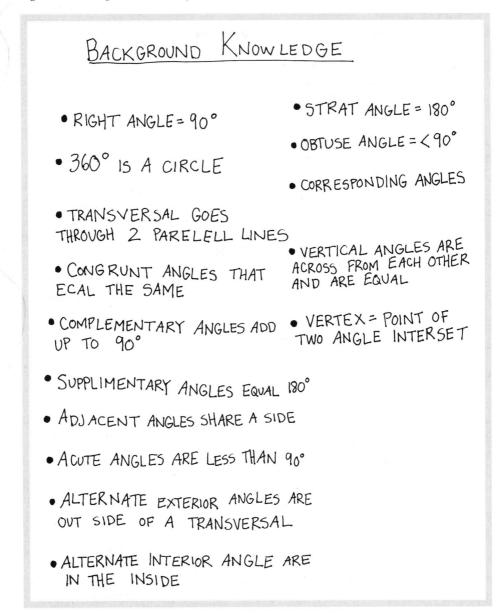

BACKGROUND KNOWLEDGE

- RIGHT ANGLE = 90°

- 360° IS A CIRCLE

- TRANSVERSAL GOES THROUGH 2 PARELELL LINES

- CONGRUNT ANGLES THAT ECAL THE SAME

- COMPLEMENTARY ANGLES ADD UP TO 90°

- SUPPLIMENTARY ANGLES EQUAL 180°

- ADJACENT ANGLES SHARE A SIDE

- ACUTE ANGLES ARE LESS THAN 90°

- ALTERNATE EXTERIOR ANGLES ARE OUT SIDE OF A TRANSVERSAL

- ALTERNATE INTERIOR ANGLE ARE IN THE INSIDE

- STRAT ANGLE = 180°

- OBTUSE ANGLE = < 90°

- CORRESPONDING ANGLES

- VERTICAL ANGLES ARE ACROSS FROM EACH OTHER AND ARE EQUAL

- VERTEX = POINT OF TWO ANGLE INTERSET

In *Comprehending Math*, Art Hyde (2006) documented the ways in which he and a group of math teachers developed and presented these thinking strategies to math learners, and today, teachers and students are finding new and interesting ways that these strategies can serve to help us make meaning of mathematics.

Mathematicians can utilize these strategies as readers of content, problem solvers, and critical thinkers. More information on each strategy and how they might be used by math learners is offered in Appendix A, but for now, the table on page 30 introduces us to the meaning of each strategy and how it might sound at work in the classroom.

These strategies are far more than sentence stems and conversation starters, but rather learned approaches that can scaffold students' independence as problem solvers. We as teachers can surely solicit students' background knowledge before delving into a new unit, but, more importantly, we can explicitly name and teach this practice as something learners can do automatically and independently when they meet with a challenge: ask themselves, "What do I already know about this?" More details on each strategy and how it might serve math learners are offered in Appendix A.

The thinking strategies themselves offer us concrete means toward the broad goals established by the Common Core and Partnership for 21st Century Skills: When we expect students to, for example, "Construct viable arguments and critique the reasoning of others" (the third mathematical practice articulated by the Common Core), they need to know *how*. The thinking strategies present the very means to that end: determining importance and asking questions, to begin. Or, when it comes to Creativity and Innovation, the thinking strategies offer learners a menu of approaches that can support their progress: drawing on background knowledge, making mental models, and monitoring for meaning. Because, of these three lists, the thinking strategies offer the most specific and practical inroads to understanding, they are featured in numerous classroom vignettes throughout the book.

Now you have three sets of tools: Common Core mathematical practices, twenty-first-century skills, and thinking strategies. On top of your content standards, this could feel like an avalanche of unhelpful fluff. But if we take seriously the imperative that students need tools for independent problem solving, not just answers, these three lists offer us a wonderful array of implements we can hand over to learners as tools to assist them in leveraging student understanding of content for themselves.

Teaching the Tools

We want to teach learners to think and reason independently, and we have this wonderful set of tools to help them. Our job is not to use the strategies to become better mathematicians and explainers ourselves, but rather to model and transfer the strategies to students so that they can carry them and select from them as needed, just as a master painter opens up his kit and selects the precise brush he needs for a canvas in progress. The forum for apprenticeship of this sort is the workshop model. For any given learning sequence, we can identify a content learning target coupled with an appropriate process learning goal, one that will support not only students' learning in a specific unit, but also students' growth as mathematicians over time.

For example, in planning a seventh-grade unit on writing equations, I might elect to work on the first practice: make sense of problems and persevere in solving them, which is closely akin to the twenty-first-century skill, problem solving, and critical thinking. To this end, I am going to focus in on mental models as a specific thinking strategy I can teach that will offer learners a useful tool for problem solving. Here is a brief lesson plan for one day's workshop.

More details on each phase of a workshop model lesson are offered in later chapters. My point here is merely to model that intentional planning for both content and process learning targets at each stage of the workshop can ensure that students not only understand math concepts but also learn to use transferable tools that will help them problem solve beyond the confines of prealgebra.

	Content	**Process**
Learning Goals	Write equations from word problems.	Use mental models (problem solving).
Minilesson	◆ I introduce equations. ◆ I model translating a mental model into an equation.	◆ I introduce mental models as a means to represent mathematical situations. ◆ We discuss a variety of possible strategies for modeling. ◆ We read a word problem and explore various mental models that could be used to illustrate the situation.
Work Time	◆ Students read word problems, create mental models to represent those situations, then translate those into equations.	
Sharing and Reflection	◆ Students share solutions. ◆ Students discuss which strategies make the most sense to them.	◆ Students write short reflections on how mental models helped them to write equations.

So this should just be a math lesson for one day?

"Yeah, but . . . "

"This is too much—math practices, twenty-first-century skills, thinking strategies, plus all of our district standards, benchmarks, and requirements."

It is a lot. I agree. And you do not have to do all of it at once. I suggest simply that for every content learning goal, you match a process learning goal, seeing each math benchmark as a chance to teach thinking, rather than simply to transmit a thought. They are symbiotic, mutually supportive.

"I thought the thinking strategies were for reading. What do they have to do with math?"

The research on thinking strategies did begin as research on reading. Still, the question those researchers were asking had to do with the process of coming to understand—which is a similar process regardless of what it is we are studying, be it Pythagoras, physics, poetry, or polemics. As learners, we use strategies to make sense of ideas, and those strategies can be useful across content areas, with some modifications.

Quod Erat Demonstrandum

This chapter is based on the belief that we can teach students how to think and succeed as mathematicians, and that to do so we need to impart to them specific practices, skills, and strategies that will support their success. Most broadly, the Common Core standards for mathematical practice and twenty-first-century skills can guide our process learning goals, and the thinking strategies offer specific, concrete habits of mind students can employ as readers, thinkers, and problem solvers seeking to comprehend content. To teach each of these, we need to apprentice learners in their use in the craft of building mathematical understanding. Minds-on math workshops are an ideal forum for teaching learners how to employ these thinking tools.

CHAPTER 3

Tasks

The truth is that in many areas of the subject, mathematics has as much to do with computation as writing has to do with typing.

– John Allen Paulos, **Innumeracy: Mathematical Illiteracy and Its Consequences**

Problem of the Day: How can we design math learning activities that generate student understanding?

Postulate: When we believe in students' agency and efficacy as mathematicians, we prioritize time for learners to grapple with high cognitive demand tasks that catalyze their understanding of important mathematical ideas.

Fifth period, I am observing a seventh-grade math class: each pair of students is rolling two six-sided dice, multiplying their face values, then recording whether their product is odd or even. Twenty times. I ask Noe and Vanessa to show me the game. He rolls a three and a six; she writes those numbers down on the blanks in the next line of her worksheet. Vanessa looks at the times table in the back of her composition book, locates their product, then writes down "eighteen" on her paper. Noe copies that number onto his worksheet. She asks him if it's odd or even. "Odd," he decides.

"How do you know?" I ask.

Well trained in the system of guess and check, he scans my face for clues and immediately changes his answer: "Even."

"Why?" I probe.

"I don't know," he confesses, shrugging his shoulders.

"What does it mean to be even?" I ask them both. Blank.

Flummoxed, Noe reaches out for help. "Mister!" he calls over to his teacher, "What is even?"

The teacher waves to the board, "Ends in zero, two, four, six, or eight. Check the list on the board."

Noe looks back over at me, "Even means it's on the board."

The crux of a minds-on math workshop is the work time; the crux of the work time is the task. In this chapter, we will consider the design of tasks that promote mathematical thinking and catalyze conceptual understanding.

Let us start by considering what Noe and Vanessa are really being asked to do: First, they roll the dice. Then, they write down the numbers. Then, she looks up their product on the multiplication table, and they write that down. Next, they look at the digit in the product's ones place and check whether that digit is in the list on the board. Then they write a word: *odd* or *even*. To complete this task, these learners need to know how to use their tools—dice, table, list, pencil, and paper. But what are Noe and Vanessa being asked to *think* about, *talk* about, and *understand*? Very little: how to locate numbers in a times table, how to fill in a worksheet—skills they probably grasped years ago. And they will do them correctly. And get all their points.

But what will they understand? Noe thinks *even* means being on the board. What's going to happen when someone erases the board?

These learners are not being asked to wrestle with the principles—the big ideas— behind this work: probability when rolling a die, what multiplication represents, the notion that even numbers can be divided by two into equal integers. They are not being asked to create, problem solve, or negotiate. They are not being asked to think.

Noe and Vanessa are trapped on the surface. Without opportunities to dive deep and understand the ideas supporting the work that they are expected to do, they miss the chance to exercise their good minds to grapple with the concepts. Vanessa and Noe are left to play along like trained monkeys, going through the motions of math, recording correct answers, but robbed of the meaning behind the numbers. This is the problem of shallow math.

Shallow Math

Perhaps you are familiar with this task and others like it that can be found in popular textbooks. Vanessa and Noe are not alone. In math classes across the country, learners are expected to memorize algorithms and apply them, complete hunt and copy exercises, plug and chug numbers without considering the questions: So what? Why are we doing this? What does this number or equation or concept really *mean*?

Although reform-minded curricula often offer a departure from silent seatwork to embrace more collaborative activities, too many of our students are still simply hunting for right answers, rather than seeking to make meaning of ideas. It reminds me of my own experience as a learner in an early Spanish class—we had to memorize and then recite two-voice dialogues in front of the group; we could get a good grade for pronouncing all the words correctly, regardless of whether we understood the meaning.

Textbooks and other classroom materials cannot be held responsible for keeping us in the shallows. To ensure for all learners a bright mathematical future, we must find ways to take them deeper, far enough into the heart of the work to understand what math really means and why it means anything at all. In this chapter, we will explore how.

Deep Math

Students need opportunities to sink their teeth into the marrow of math. Challenge is engaging, exciting, exhausting, and inspiring. We may wince at the thought of pushing learners out of their comfort zones or of posing a problem whose answer mystifies even us. Yet, to do justice to Noe and Vanessa's good minds, we must be courageous and take the plunge. Let's explore the meaning of and the means to promote deep math.

I asked a first grader to explain even numbers. "It's a number where every number inside it has a partner," he began. "Like six," he said holding up three fingers on each hand, then matching up the fingers on one hand with the three on the other. "Six is even because you can divide it up, and every number has a partner." He poked his fingers at each other. "See? Even."

"How about nine?" I asked.

He reorganized his fingers, producing a hand with one thumb folded in, the other hand with all five digits extended. "Nope. Not even." He wiggled his lonely thumb at me. "Odd."

This child defines even numbers by a quality, a way that you can test for them: Break it in two, and see if the parts match up. He has a mental model—matching up pairs—that he utilizes to demonstrate his understanding. Although he left out some nuance that an older mathematician might incorporate into her answer, this first grader has an operative grasp on the concept, an understanding he can build upon throughout his career as a math learner. This is deep math. Deep math is rooted from and culminates in understanding, a recursive process. Deep math needs to be the focal point of our minds-on math workshops.

The Role of Challenging Tasks in a Minds-on Math Workshop

A minds-on math workshop looks different from a typical day trudging through the text. Let's just take a glimpse at what it means to center your math workshop around a well-tuned task:

Invited several years ago to teach a "demonstration" lesson to an algebra II class at a Colorado high school, I selected a juicy task that could raise most misconceptions about the meaning of each variable in a parabola's equation. After talking with the group about documenting our thinking while working, I invited students to find the intersection of two parabolas based on their equations and to explain their solution both graphically and in numbers. Students worked independently, and then we moved into a group discussion about their solutions; seven distinct answers emerged. Rather than identifying the right one and flushing the rest, I facilitated a discussion in which the students struggled to make sense of which proposed solution was correct and why.

Our discourse fueled passions and generated confusion. We spent a long time discussing, asking questions, voting, explaining, and revisiting. Everyone was arguing, thinking, writing, curious to know which was correct and why. It took the whole period. Before the bell rang, I gave students each a half-sheet of paper and asked them to write about what they understood about parabolas now and also what they were still wondering about.

After this "demonstration" lesson, the host teacher was acutely distressed. "How can you justify spending a whole period on a single parabola!?" she begged to know. Highly concerned about the significant pressure for coverage in her school and district, she did not feel she could possibly justify so much time devoted to solving a single problem.

My subsequent conversation with her included many of the points in this chapter:

• Understanding, not coverage, ought to be our goal as teachers.

• Challenging tasks generate and demonstrate understanding.

• We need to devote our class time to making meaning of those juicy tasks to cultivate comprehension.

This shift from pursuing content coverage to seeking student understanding is a critical change we must make in our beliefs about math instruction. We want learners up to their knees in the murky swamp of mathematical ideas, pushing aside the weeds, fighting toward the sunlight of understanding, on a quest. Struggle is central to growth; when we wrestle to make sense, our hard-won comprehension will not easily be lost or forgotten.

In order for students' mathematical experiences to challenge them and catalyze their understanding, we need to provide some evocative material for learners to think about—this is why juicy problems are central to your minds-on math workshop.

Learning Goals

Although state standards, district benchmarks, and school curricula channel our efforts, teachers' goals for students vary. I remember that in my first few weeks of classroom teaching, my goals included things like not having anything thrown at me and students being busy enough that no fights broke out in my room. Eventually, my goals for students progressed to include things like actually finishing the Pythagoras unit before winter break, and finally to hopes of learners truly understanding the meaning behind the math.

My goals dictated the sorts of tasks I asked students to complete: When I was after silent, noncombative seatwork, I served up word searches. Once I went for unit completion, tasks included review packets full of problems that looked just like what would be on the test (only with different numbers). Eventually, the tasks I invited learners to engage with during math work time evolved to include opportunities for students to wrestle with complex problems that revealed their understanding of important mathematical ideas.

Our goals drive our task design. When saddled with a four-hundred-page algebra book or an expectation of completing eight units before the state test, sincere teachers often fall for the myth that "coverage" is achievement. Our wise mentors Wiggins and McTighe, in their important work *Understanding by Design* (1998), remind us of the "twin sins" of typical instruction: activities-based (word search) and coverage-oriented (unit review packet). They encourage us to cast these aside in favor, instead, of the more elusive goal of content understanding. This approach does not mean we relinquish the responsibility of covering standards; rather, we relieve ourselves of the notion that we and our students must read every page and do every problem in the text. When the goal is understanding, not completion, we can be flexible in selecting how we use our work and instructional time, choosing to milk those tasks that take us deepest.

To plan for understanding, we must ask ourselves, "If my students really understood the concepts I want them to understand, what would they be able to *do*?" For adding and subtracting positive and negative integers, some options might be:

a. Use a calculator correctly.

b. Solve a worksheet full of integer problems (5 + −3).

c. Explain how to balance a checkbook.

d. Design and create an illustrated user's guide explaining the pitfalls of adding and subtracting operations with positive and negative numbers.

e. All of the above.

Of course, you could argue for any of these as plausible demonstrations of understanding. Think for a moment about what a student's ability to complete any one of these tasks might show you about what she did and did not "get" about operations with positive and negative numbers.

Figure 3.1   *How does this student demonstrate understanding?*

Display and tell what you know about transversal & congruent angles!

congruent

What we know: They are the same measure.

* They are in transversal angles.

same measure

transversal

What we know:

* Creates congruent angles.

* Are lines that cut across a set of parallel lines.

45° 135°
135° 45°

45° 135°
135° 45°

Cognitive Demand

The 1999 Trends in Mathematics and Science Study comparing thirty industrialized nations found that "high-performing countries avoided reducing mathematics tasks to mere procedural exercises involving basic computational skills, and they placed greater cognitive demands on students by encouraging them to focus on concepts and connections among those concepts in their problem-solving" (Resnick 2006).

To help us think about what sorts of tasks might invite and yield deep understanding, we can look to academics' conversations about cognitive demand, or degree of intellectual difficulty. "If we want students to develop the capacity to think, reason, and problem solve, then we need to start with high-level, cognitively complex tasks," state Stein and Lane (1996), encouraging teachers to challenge students at higher levels across the curriculum.

In "Depth-of-Knowledge Levels for Four Content Areas," Norman Webb (2002), senior scientist at the Wisconsin Center for Educational Research, describes the

Figure 3.2 *Cognitive Demand of Mathematical Tasks*

Level	Description	Sample Instructions
1	**Recall** • of fact, definition, term • simple procedure, algorithm, or formula • rote response	"Identify" "Use" "Measure"
2	**Skill/concept** • some decision making or mental processing required • interpreting information • displaying data in graphs, tables	"Solve" "Organize" "Estimate" "Make observations" "Interpret data"
3	**Strategic thinking** • requires reasoning, planning, citing evidence • make conjectures, justify responses • using concepts to solve problems and explain phenomena	"Explain" "Justify"
4	**Extend thinking** • complex reasoning, planning, development • making connections between ideas within or across content areas	"Design and conduct" "Synthesize" "Critique"

range of cognitive demand invited by mathematical tasks. Figure 3.2 summarizes his work.

In the third column of this table, you will see familiar terms from Bloom's taxonomy (Bloom et al. 1956). Webb goes on to explain how similar-looking tasks can offer varied levels of demand: "If a student has to take the water temperature from a river each day for a month and then construct a graph, this would be classified as a Level 2. However, if the student is to conduct a river study that requires taking into consideration a number of variables, this would be a Level 4."

So, if our goal is students' deep understanding of mathematical ideas, our duty is to provide them with tasks of high cognitive demand. Tough tasks alone are not a guarantor of student learning; we must ensure that our own role as facilitators enhances, rather than detracts from, the demand of those tasks. We need to ask good questions, promote connections to prior knowledge, and encourage conceptual thinking rather than rescuing students from struggle by simplifying problems or offering algorithms to follow. In later chapters, we will explore other elements critical to exploring math deeply: how teachers "set up" a task in a carefully planned minilesson (Chapter 6), and the ways in which high-level discourse can enhance student understanding (Chapter 5).

Changing Tasks

If you are fortunate, you are feeling very confident now that your curricular materials provide for your students a high level of cognitive demand; you have an increased depth of understanding about why that cognitive demand is important, and you know that you need not rescue students from their struggles.

If you are less fortunate, you are thinking that the notion of high cognitive demand makes sense and that you would love to find some problems that offer your students just that.

As you have probably observed, many of our commercially produced math programs offer tasks at an array of levels within each chapter: Noe and Vanessa, mentioned earlier, were completing a page right from the class text. In another chapter of that same book, students are asked to apply their knowledge of integers to solve multilayered real-world problems that certainly required a depth of understanding. Unfortunately, the really juicy tasks are often printed at the tail end of each chapter, and too often we "run out" of time for them.

Sometimes when I coach teachers about prioritizing student thinking and understanding, they may realize that the curriculum and materials used in their building only infrequently invite students to grapple intellectually at the level we might hope. In these instances, teachers might feel concerned that they are not "allowed" to

High Cognitive Demand: What to Look For

- Multiple entry points: Students with varying levels of prior knowledge could access the problem.

- Various possible approaches: Although the problem may have only one correct answer, there are numerous possible ways to find that answer.

- Higher-order thinking required: Students need to think critically and understand the conceptual basis behind the problem, rather than simply insert numbers in a formula.

- Opportunities to synthesize: Problem invites students to draw together background knowledge about various strands of mathematics, as well as relate mathematics to the real world.

- Justification and explanation: Requires solution to be explained or applied in one or more ways.

Example: Alexis and her sister Jasmine are both members of the school's fifteen-player basketball team. To give everyone chances to get to know each other, their coach likes to assign seats randomly when they travel to games. This week, three parents are driving in their minivans. Each minivan can carry five players, three in the middle row and two in the back row. If Coach draws names from a hat and assigns seats, what are the chances that the two sisters will end up side by side? Explain your answer in two or more of the following ways: numbers, words, pictures, models.

Note: Context is a key strategy for promoting motivation and engagement. Students enjoy doing math problems that they can relate to, where the real-world application of the content is clear. Beware, though, that writing every word problem about spicy hot Cheetos could be setting learners up for a fall: In the world of standardized testing and textbook manufacturers, learners are expected to engage in and comprehend mathematical tasks that may have nothing whatsoever to do with their daily life. They therefore need practice solving problems related to both relevant and irrelevant situations.

change their curriculum. Although in some instances, this has indeed been the case, most often, school administrators and district officers are intent that the *learning goals* of the program be accomplished in a given time frame and are less attached to the exact problem sets and page numbers utilized to accomplish that goal.

For example, Ms. Tingley knew she had to get through the percents unit in five weeks and have her sixth graders ready for the benchmark assessment at the end of the semester. For years, her department had used their textbooks, marching through each lesson in the chapter in time to be done and "ready" for the exam. When she started to lean back from the text and pick out the important concepts in the chapter that students needed to understand, she was able to pull out tasks of high cognitive demand and part with rote ones, dedicating learning time and energy to build conceptual understanding. Rather than puzzling through extensive worksheets calculating sale prices of various items given various discounts, she asked students to each choose a real-world problem and create an extensive explanation of how they solved it—including words, pictures, base ten grid squares, and mathematical calculations. She invited learners to evaluate and assess the solutions of their peers and to reflect on why percents were important to understand. In this way, she supported students in not only making sense of the content but also honing the problem-solving skills that held them in good stead when the state test came to town.

Our responsibility as teachers is to prioritize the tasks of high cognitive demand that *do* appear in our curricula and to find ways to capitalize on those to facilitate students' conceptual understanding. We also need to be vigilant when the cognitive demand lags; when it does, we have three options:

- resequencing existing tasks
- modifying existing tasks
- finding better tasks.

Next, I elaborate on each.

Resequencing Existing Tasks

In her quest to identify meaty tasks that could serve at the heart of math workshops, middle school math teacher Angela Zehner observed that often high cognitive demand tasks could be found at the very end of each textbook chapter, and sometimes in the extension activities. You know the ones—those multilayered real-world problems asking students to use what they know about scientific notation to calculate the distance between Mars and Jupiter knowing only how far each is from our sun.

Aware of research presented by Hiebert in *Making Sense* (1997) stating that the "level and kind of thinking in which students engage determines what they will learn," Zehner pulled those challenging tasks to the forefront in her classroom, using them to launch units rather than as challenges only for students who completed other work.

Savvy teachers intentionally pluck these tasks out and feature them front and center. Even if students are not quite ready to solve these juicy problems at the get-go, the problems themselves create a "need to know" that makes the entire unit's content relevant. Take a peek into the end of your book's chapters, or the sidebars of your teachers' materials, and you are likely to find some gems. In Chapters 6 through 9, we will discuss how the workshop framework, built around a great task, can be used to catapult students forward in their thinking and understanding.

Modifying Existing Tasks

If your materials do not seem to provide the sort of amazing problems you are looking for, you may have to take the bull by the horns and create some of your own. Before you start getting the idea that you need to rewrite your math book, let me assure you that a little goes a long way. If you set a modest goal of ensuring a couple of high cognitive demand tasks in each week and work with teammates to locate or develop those, you will hone your craft at refining math problems, and next year you'll find it even easier to raise the ante. Fear not!

You can start with typical problems you find in your text, resource materials, and files. Then, here are some possible approaches to increasing the cognitive demand of the tasks you *already* have:

- increase complexity
- introduce ambiguity
- synthesize strands of mathematics
- invite conceptual connections
- require explanation and justification
- propose solutions that reveal misconceptions or common errors.

We could take one or more of these approaches to modifying an existing task, while remaining vigilant to stay true to the understanding goal. Let us consider an example:

Typical Problem: Mavis the cow is tethered to the outside corner of a square barn on a ten foot rope. How large is her grazing area?

Understanding Goal: Find the area of a fractional part of a circle.

Modification	Definition	Sample Revision
Increase complexity	Add layers of challenge, possibly including additional steps, a need to work backward.	If we want to tether Mavis the cow to the outside corner of a square barn and give her a grazing area of five hundred square feet, how long would her rope need to be?
Introduce ambiguity	Offer incomplete information requiring problem solvers to draw inferences, ask questions.	If we tether Mavis the cow to the corner of a barn on a twelve-foot rope, how much grazing area will she have?*
Synthesize strands of mathematics	Comingle geometry, algebra, probability, statistics, number sense, etc.	Rope costs $1.50 a meter, and you have $10 to spend on a tether for Mavis the cow. We plan to tether her to the outside corner of your square barn. How big will her grazing area be?

Invite conceptual connections	Ask big picture questions requiring learners to link their current studies with other work in mathematics.	Mavis the cow is tethered to the outside corner of a square barn on a ten-foot rope. Calculate her grazing area. Then, using this problem as an example, describe the similarities and differences between the ways that algebra and geometry help us solve problems.
Require explanation and justification	Invite students to defend their thinking in various ways: visually, graphically, numerically, kinesthetically, etc.	Mavis the cow is tethered to an outside corner of a square barn on a nine-foot rope. If you needed to pave her range with one-foot square concrete slabs, how many would you need? Justify your solution in two or more ways.
Propose solutions	Offer an answer to a problem, and ask students to evaluate its correctness and explain their assessment.	Allison calculated that if Mavis the cow were tethered to the outside corner of a square barn on a ten-foot rope, she would have 314 square feet of area to graze. Is she correct? Why or why not?

*The ambiguities are many here: What shape is the barn? Is she inside or outside? How big is the barn? Is all of her range grazing? Rather than answer these questions for problem solvers directly, we can invite their logical thinking by responding to their questions with questions: What do you think? Could you solve it different ways? Which would make the most sense? Ask students to take a reasoned stance and to back it up.

Which problem would you rather solve? Might your students have similar opinions? Here is another way to increase cognitive demand: Offer students choice in which problems they tackle within a given set of high cognitive demand problems around a common learning goal, and then invite them to talk about what makes certain sorts of problems more appealing or accessible to them than others. Another opportunity to justify and explain.

The problems you already have are a great starting point, and you will surely find strategies beyond the six I offer here to help you challenge students in deeper ways. (A further sampling of juicy problems is available in Appendix B.)

Finding Better Tasks

Then there are the days when inspiration does not strike! If modifying existing problems feels daunting, Appendix B lists some resources that might serve up juicy

Bloom's Taxonomy

The New Bloom's Taxonomy, a revised version that replaced "comprehension" with "understanding" as the second level of knowing, is another useful tool inviting us to analyze the mental work a certain task is inviting students to do. The highest cognitive demand tasks are, according to this framework, at the top of the pyramid.

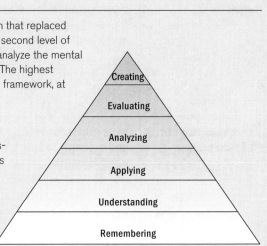

According to Benjamin Bloom and his successors, the lower level of the pyramid represents the most elementary intellectual tasks, while, as we approach its peak, cognitive demand increases. To help us envision what this organizing structure could mean for math teachers, let us walk through Bloom's levels in reverse order, as though climbing the pyramid:

(Overbaugh and Schultz n.d.)

Taxonomic Level	Definition	Math Example
Remembering	Recall information.	What is a^0?
Understanding	Make meaning of a concept for one's self.	Explain why a^0 is 1.
Applying	Use knowledge in a new context.	Solve $a^3 \times a^0$.
Analyzing	Study the component parts of a concept, problem, or solution.	Explain your answer to $a^3 \times a^0$.
Evaluating	Judge the accuracy or utility of an answer or idea.	Assess whether this is correct, and discuss why: $a^3 \times a^3 \times a^2 = a^5 \times a^2 \times a^0$.
Creating	Make something new and unique that interprets an important concept in a novel way.	Develop a memorable mental model explaining positive, negative, and zero exponents.

Regardless of whose taxonomy or definitions we choose to embrace, most important is that we as teachers create learning experiences that challenge our students to stretch and grow the muscles of their minds. These experiences begin with offering challenging tasks that invite learners to work in their zone of proximal development; beyond the task, our role as facilitators is also of critical importance: We need to ensure that we scaffold thinking rather than rescuing learners from struggle as they pursue solutions. More on the critical role of the teacher in facilitating mathematical understanding is presented in Chapter 9, Conferring.

tasks for your students to wrestle. No matter what the source, you will still have to analyze the problems through the lens of high cognitive demand. Does the problem offer all of the following?

- multiple entry points
- various possible approaches
- a need for higher-order thinking
- opportunities to synthesize, justify, and explain

Often learners can do more than we think they can, once we provide them with the tools, community of learners, and the time to think.

"Yeah, but . . ."

"Who has time to track down or generate all these challenging problems?"

Teachers never seem to have enough time to manage all of their responsibilities. Still, when we make an effort to adjust our instruction by increasing the cognitive demand of the tasks we offer learners, the payoffs in student achievement and engagement are tremendous.

Start small. Invite colleagues to help you make adjustments. With practice, you will become efficient at developing or locating these worthy tasks, and your files will spill over with options.

"Not all my students are ready for 'high cognitive demand.'"

Although students may have experienced varying levels of success in math in the past, to support all students' achievement, we need to both raise the bar high and offer ample scaffolding toward their success. In this chapter, I discussed some of the ways in which you can raise the bar by offering challenging materials. Throughout the remainder of the book, you will read about how teacher and peer modeling, classroom discourse, and reflection can serve as strong scaffolding set on a foundation of high expectations.

"How will I know students get it if I only give one or two problems?"

Although one or two juicy problems can be the crux of a workshop, these problems need not stand alone as the sole data point to assess student understanding. We can also include additional problem sets, homework tasks, quizzes, exit tickets, as well as information gleaned from classroom conversations to inform our assessment of students' progress.

"What is a worthy task for some learners may be way too easy for others!"

As described by Carol Ann Tomlinson (Tomlinson and McTighe 2006), there are a number of ways that a wise teacher can differentiate, and workshop model instruction lends itself well to all of these. We can adjust the content, process, product, or learning environment. Though we may offer students different tasks and responsibilities during work time, students can still benefit from hearing peers' strategies, as well as reflecting together on their growth as mathematicians during the last segment of the workshop time. Differentiation will be discussed in greater depth in Chapter 8.

Quod Erat Demonstrandum

Challenging tasks require students to wrestle with ideas and cement their understanding of the content at hand. Given the purpose of minds-on math workshops as generating student understanding—their ability to remember and apply a concept to novel situations—we need to take care to prioritize time for challenging tasks. Tasks of this nature can be found in a variety of sources, as well as created by teachers adjusting existing problems. Juicy tasks sit at the heart of the workshop's design, and their use will be discussed further in later chapters.

CHAPTER 4

Community

To "manage" students' behavior, to make them do what we say, doesn't promote community or compassion, responsibility or reflection. The only way to reach those goals is to give up some control, to facilitate the tricky, noisy, maddening, unpredictable process whereby students work together to decide what respect means or how to be fair.

—*Alfie Kohn*, Beyond Discipline

Problem of the Day: How can we cultivate communities of thinkers that catalyze math learning?

Postulate: Students learn best as participants in communities of thinkers that challenge, support, and appreciate all for their contributions to the understanding of the group.

Mr. Goodman is exhausted and hoarse at the end of every day trying to get students to do something during math class. After he lets them work on the day starter problem, no one volunteers to share their answer, so he explains it. After he teaches his lesson describing again that slope is the coefficient of x, rise over run, he assigns a problem set and gives students permission to drag their desks into clusters. The district administrators want to see collaborative learning when they come for their walk-throughs. A group near the board slips into muffled conversation about weekend plans; a few cell phones appear under the desktops; pencils break, and students clump at the sharpener, slowly grinding away at their writing utensils, chatting. Mr. Goodman moves from table to table, noticing little progress being made on the problem set, prodding. "David, point to the slope in that equation . . . right, negative three, so, why does your graph have a positive slope?"

"People," he raises his voice and announces to all. "Slope is always the coefficient of x." He taps at his sample equation on the board. "Right HERE. Get to work." Students continue to chat, text, and sleep until the bell rings. "Any questions?" he invites. No one signals. "Finish this for homework," he calls out, then mutters to himself, "I know you won't." They slam their binders shut and skulk down the hall. "I hate math," one student declares as her tired teacher turns to his coffeemaker.

Teaching can be exhausting. Students can be lazy. Math can be hard. For so many reasons beyond teachers' control, learners may struggle to make the most of the opportunities lain before them. Yet regardless of our students' socioeconomic status, family composition, language proficiency, or past achievement in math, our duty is to find ways to reach them, to motivate and engage them to both care about and learn mathematics.

To this end, we need to establish growth-minded communities of thinkers optimistic about their promise as mathematicians. As described by John Van deWalle,

> A worthwhile goal is to transform your classroom into what might be termed a "mathematical community of learners," or an environment in which students interact with each other and with the teacher. In such an environment, students share ideas and results, compare and evaluate strategies, challenge results, determine the validity of answers, and negotiate ideas on which all can agree. The rich interaction in such a classroom significantly raises the chances that productive reflective thinking about relevant mathematical ideas will happen. (Van deWalle and Lovin 2006, 5)

Creating classrooms of this nature is a matter of vision and intention, as well as strategic planning and dogged persistence. The purpose of this chapter is to support you in enhancing your own plan for cultivating communities of thinkers of this sort.

Imagine leaving work inspired, rather than bone tired.

Collaboration Promotes Understanding

Humans are social animals. We like to think and talk and work together. Research points to the value of harnessing our innate propensity to engage with others in the service of math learning.

Numerous studies synthesized by researcher John Hattie in his meta-analysis *Visible Learning* (2009) point to the power of cooperative learning to enhance student achievement. As compared to individualistic learning, he found, cooperative learning had a medium to high effect on student achievement. Referring to research by Roseth, Johnson, and Johnson (2006), Hattie explained, "Under cooperative conditions, interpersonal relationships have the strongest influence on achievement, and this clearly points to the value of friendship in the achievement equation" (214).

Further, for our culturally and linguistically diverse students, a population growing rapidly across the country, recent research indicates the significant contribution of classroom communities of support to student learning (Gonzales 2005).

The value of collaborative learning in math was ably demonstrated through the work of Dr. Uri Treisman, once director of the Professional Development Program at University of California, Berkeley. He found that student achievement in mathematics is greatly enhanced by learners' working together on highly challenging material in the context of supportive study groups. Dr. Treisman's work began as a response to the problem of high calculus dropout rates among African American college freshmen at his university. Though his inquiry revealed a number of contributing factors, Dr. Treisman honed in on one distinct feature of the study habits of high-achieving Chinese American freshmen: In addition to studying independently, these students came together frequently in self-directed study groups to share their thinking and critique the work of their peers. Based on these students' success, Treisman developed a structured learning program for students from historically underachieving groups, inviting them to regularly participate in informal, nongraded group learning in a supportive setting. The majority of their weekly work time was devoted to challenging problems and peer discussion, with emphasis on understanding and explaining their work.

Twenty-First-Century Skills: Communication and Collaboration

Communities of learners are ideal proving grounds for the twenty-first-century skills of communication and collaboration. When we explicitly introduce these skills and discuss their importance not only in math class but also in life beyond the classroom walls, we offer students practical tools to prepare for the future.

Are They Really Ready to Work?, a report based on data gathered from four hundred employers across the country (Conference Board et al. 2006), describes and predicts a number of work force trends: When ranking basic knowledge as well as applied skills, CEOs predominantly agreed that the three greatest assets a young person can bring to the workplace are

+ professionalism/work ethic
+ teamwork/collaboration
+ oral communications.

I often refer to a research study completed by a Canadian government team in the late 1980s, which found at that time the number one reason that people lost their jobs was not for lack of computation, writing, or computer skills, but because they were unable to get along with colleagues. At intervals in our math instruction, we can pause and specifically remind students that they are rehearsing these life skills—cooperation and collaboration—that they can use regardless of which field they may choose to pursue in the future.

On the whole, study group members started the year "behind" in math, but their participation in the initiative catapulted their achievement beyond that of peers who were not part of the study group program. The average SAT score of Treisman's study group members was 140 points below the average for nonparticipants; still those study group students, as a group, attained an average grade of 2.6 (on a 4.0 scale) for the calculus course while their non–study group counterparts' average grade was 1.9.

This intervention ably demonstrated that the learning context and process can play a significant role in boosting student achievement. If UC Berkeley could use a study group structure to turn around a generation of would-be engineers, how can we create and sustain similar learning environments to foster success among all of the young mathematicians in our charge?

Fostering Communities of Thinkers

A learning community is a *culture*, not a *structure*. What matters most is not how we arrange the tables and chairs or assign the groups, but how we create that invisible classroom landscape that provides intellectual safety and camaraderie, promotes serious academic pursuit, and celebrates acuity of complex content.

You have been there—the classroom where a student trips and falls, and, unprompted, a peer leans down to help him pick up his papers. No one laughs. Glimpse the mathematical equivalent: Ryan is at the board in front of the class doing his level best to calculate the area of a patio minus a fountain but cannot quite grasp the answer. Chantel offers a suggestion, "I see you working it with numbers. Can you try drawing the setup?" No one laughs. No one talks. Everyone watches and thinks while Ryan puzzles through, then the group discusses, recommends the inclusion of correct units, and applauds his final answer. The teacher remains silently perched at the back counter, inserting a comment now and again.

How do we cultivate such a community in our classrooms? As with all teaching, building community begins with a *belief*—the belief that all students can and should see each other as allies on their learning journey, and that we as teachers can be powerful agents in creating thriving communities of thinkers.

Some teachers I visit or coach express dismay about the existing learning culture in their classrooms: Students filibuster instruction, distract themselves with electronics, heckle peers, harass teachers, fall mute, or simply put their heads down on their desks to await the bell. You can picture the scene.

And although most teachers agree in theory with the *idea* of nurturing a thriving community of thinkers, many argue the impracticality of devoting time to orchestrating such a learning environment given one or more of the following: pressure to cover the content; lack of resources; lack of planning time; past failures to successfully implement cooperative learning; and more. . . . All of these challenges are real, yet worth overcoming for the sake of student learning.

You *can* craft a culture. Jaime Escalante did it. So did Louanne Johnson and Joe Clark, as have numerous other teachers whose names we may never know. And you can, too. Following are some strategies.

To create community of any sort—not merely of math learners—I observe a need for three key ingredients:

- intention—develop a vision and working purposefully toward that

- interdependence—emphasize opportunities for learners to co-create

- homeostasis—balance all socioemotional forces as they shift and change.

Under each of these broader approaches, there are numerous strategies to try. Let's take a look.

Intention

There is an old story about an eagle that, as a young eaglet, somehow ended up living with chickens in their coop. She ate, played, and slept like a chicken for a long time, not recognizing any difference between herself and the birds around her. When finally someone came to realize that this bird was, in fact, an eagle, and invited her to stretch forth her wings and fly, the poor bird had no idea what to do. All she had ever done was behave like a chicken, and no one had ever asked more of her.

On the importance of establishing a community, veteran teacher and teacher educator Ron Berger explains, "Students adjust their attitudes and efforts in order to fit into the culture. If the peer culture ridicules academic effort and achievement—it isn't cool to raise your hand in class, to do homework, to care openly about school—this is a powerful force. If the peer culture celebrates investment in school—it's cool to care—this is just as powerful. Schools need to consciously shape their cultures to be places where it's safe to care, where it's cool to care" (2003, 35).

The Pygmalion effect is alive and well in our classrooms. It is our duty to hold high expectations not only for student achievement but also for students' engagement as members of a quality learning community, and to purposefully and consistently convey those expectations to learners every day. Each time a child enters our room, we need to look that learner in the eye and see nothing but brilliant potential.

Establish vision.

If Ernest Shackleton's leadership could keep twenty-six marooned polar explorers alive and optimistic in subfreezing temperatures with inadequate clothing for nearly two years on a diet of seal meat and seagulls (if this allusion has lost you, I highly recommend reading up on *The Endurance*), you can certainly wrangle the will of a posse of tweens or teens tossed by the seas of fate into your classroom.

From day one, you can be explicit about your expectations and approach. "This class is a workshop. You are apprentices. Your job is to learn the craft of mathematicians, and my job is to model for and with you the thinking this work requires. Whoever does the work does the learning, and so I am planning to turn most of the thinking and talking over to you."

You will likely also need to sell to some learners the value of learning math at all, and you surely have your own justification for its value. I used to tell my students that math is like jumping jacks—there may not be a real-life application for those little tricks of hopping back and forth and waving one's arms, but through them we can learn a great many things about coordination, competence, and fitness. Similarly, math is an exercise strengthening the muscle of the mind. A strong mind is an irreplaceable treasure, one you are going to learn to cultivate. In nations around the world, education is a privilege, not a right; yet in our country, students arrive on our classrooms feeling entitled to be there and to be entertained. This classroom is going to be different.

Of course, students test us. Unaccustomed to the responsibilities you are levying upon them, learners may think they can wait you out, that if they are sufficiently lazy you will come to their rescue, as perhaps have numerous well-intentioned teachers in the past. Yet, as researchers studying footage from the 2003 *Trends in International Mathematics and Science Study* (TIMSS) video study (National Center for Education Statistics 2003) point out, for learners to develop conceptual understanding as mathematicians, we must resist the temptation to rescue them from thinking for themselves.

Talk every day about why you are there and what you hope. Back it up with action.

No doubt, establishing and maintaining your vision of an effective, engaged community of thinkers will take the dogged persistence Shackleton's team drew upon to drag three one-ton wooden lifeboats across craggy ice fields in search of open water. Difficult, yes, but not insurmountable. And well worth the struggle.

Align expectations.

Students may come in to your class assuming math will be pretty much like last year and that they will pretty much get to behave as they did last year, which may or may not be your hope for the group. Some teachers take the time to explain their own classroom expectations to students and perhaps to invite learners to sign on in

Norm	Definition	Examples
You are responsible for your own learning.	You are in the driver's seat and need to show up every day ready to engage and make the most of your learning opportunities.	Come to class well fed, with materials, without distractions (toys, cell phones, nail polish, etc.) and use your time wisely throughout.
You are responsible for supporting the learning of others.	Interact with peers in a way that builds their confidence and helps them to understand the content we are studying.	Be kind. Be encouraging. Treat people the way you would like to be treated. Respond when peers talk with you. Ask coaching questions, rather than giving answers. Invite peers to explain thinking. Affirm insight.
Be where you are supposed to be.	Show respect for yourself and the learning community by being where the learning is.	Be here on time. Stay with your group. When fetching materials, do it quickly and safely.
Take care of our learning environment.	All physical property in the classroom needs to be treated gently and stored properly.	Write only on paper or boards. Use materials appropriately and store them where they belong.

a show of agreement. A still smaller group of teachers will invest some class time inviting students to envision what an optimal learning community could look like and to collaboratively develop classroom norms that will lead them there; a time-consuming process, but one that can yield significant investment from the students in upholding the community they themselves envision. Whether you present or invite students to co-create classroom norms, the above suggestions will go a long way toward creating your thinking community.

Keep the list short. Refer to them often. Explain them. Act them out. Celebrate them happening. Talk about how they feel.

Convey confidence.

Teachers play a critical role in arranging the discursive histories from which (these) children speak. Talk is the central tool of their trade. With it, they mediate children's activity and experience and help them make sense of learning, literacy, life and themselves.

Peter Johnston, in **Choice Words:**
How Our Language Affects Children's Learning

How we speak to learners about their work and their thinking has a tremendous impact on their growth as mathematicians. Visit Rachel Rosenberg's classroom, and listen to how she talks to her students. In three minutes one morning, I heard:

"You worked really hard today to figure this out."

"I love how you are thinking about that."

"Wow! Can you explain that again? I really liked what you were saying."

"I am so impressed with your effort."

"Help us understand your good thinking."

How would you feel about yourself as a mathematician if someone talked to you like this all period? Probably a lot like Ms. Rosenberg's students—great! They work hard; they want her to catch them being smart; they want to hear their thinking celebrated. With each comment and interaction, Rachel regularly reaffirms her faith in students, and seeds the classroom culture with agency and efficacy. This growth-minded can-do belief system is alluring; everyone wants to be seen and supported; in time, more and more students fall into its grasp.

You convey your confidence in students when you:

- affirm effort: "Rory, you are working so hard on carefully recording your thinking."

- appreciate contributions: "Leticia, I like the way you helped your group to find all the materials you needed."

- celebrate thinking: "Vincent, that is a wonderful new way to think about solving this problem, using what you know about baseball batting averages."

- hold a vision for their best: "Emily, it's not like you to be so quiet in a group."

Build individual relationships.

Communities are comprised of individuals. We must therefore make every effort to enlist the engagement of each person. One of my favorite teaching stories about the importance of individual support for collective endeavor begins with three sailors adrift in a small wooden lifeboat. Late one night, one looks over to observe his compatriot drilling a hole under one of the benches. "What are you doing?!" He exclaims.

"Drilling a hole," The busy sailor answers.

"You can't do that to our boat!"

"Why not? It's under *my* seat."

In this example, we can see the obvious importance of an "all for one and one for all approach." In our classrooms, we can be similarly vigilant to those students who are reluctant to participate in the learning community. They undermine not only their own progress but also the esprit de corps of the community. Math is not a spectator sport.

Winning passive resisters' participation is a matter of will, but also a matter of time. My first year in the classroom, I inherited a group of memorable little rascals who made it their mission to mess with me at every turn. "Win the middle," my then-principal advised me: There are the students who will pretty much always cooperate, those who see their role in the classroom as disturbing the peace, and then most of our students tend to fall someplace in the middle. Your job, like any presidential candidate's, is to find ways to build rapport with the swing voters, the mass in the middle, whose agreement with your approach can make all the difference. Here are some things to try:

- Connect students' lives to the content. Eat lunch with them, catch them between classes, find out about their interests and refer to those in the context of math lessons. "As Milena knows from her study of piano, there are four-sixteenths in a quarter note. Those are equivalent fractions." Everyone likes to be seen.

- Connect with parents. Take a few minutes each day to send a few emails or leave voicemails with parents noting specific things their learner is doing well: "This is Ms. Hoffer, Max's math teacher, and I want you to know that today I was so delighted to hear him describe to the entire class how he thinks about solving combination problems." Now the parents appreciate you for finding the good in their child, and the student knows that you know how to reach his parents.

- Show that you care. This may seem obvious that we teachers care about students, but especially as learners get into middle school, they experience the environment as less personal and their teachers as more distant. Find ways to show that you see and appreciate your students. I am sure you know teachers that bring treats on test days or loan pencils without qualms or go to school sporting events or find other ways to demonstrate they care about and are interested in students. What do you do to show interest and convey support?

Control your thoughts.

Not only does every classroom have its culture, but as you well know, each faculty does as well. Too many times, I have walked into teachers' lounges to overhear a conversation about a class that was "dumb as a box of rocks" or a student who "will be working at a convenience store until he gets shot." While venting about the significant frustrations and challenges inherent in teaching can feel cathartic, when you catch yourself falling into a pessimistic belief system about individuals or groups, walk away.

Fill your mind with confident thoughts about what is possible for all learners. Your unflagging optimism, and the ways in which you demonstrate that to learners, is one of the greatest gifts a child can receive.

- Maintain an asset stance. Devote time, energy, and attention to the positive contributions of all learners, especially those hardest to appreciate. In class, if Billy is driving you crazy, look for an opportunity to catch him doing the right thing, "Thank you, Billy, for having a good sharp pencil today/putting that paper in the recycling bin/being the first one ready to listen."

- Presume positive intent. When a learner chooses not to do what is asked, assume there is a legitimate reason and venture to find out what it is. Maybe she is confused or sick or exhausted. Ask, "What is it that you need in order to engage as a learner today?"

- Cultivate compassion. If a learner missteps or reacts confrontationally, find compassion in the possibility that there may be extenuating circumstances in the child's life causing her to behave in such a way. Express concern, "You seem upset. What's going on?"

When you feel your resolve wane, get some exercise, eat some ice cream, call your mom, read *The Energy to Teach* (Graves 2001), take a sabbatical. Watch inspiring teaching movies about real-life heroes in the classroom (*Stand and Deliver*, *Dangerous Minds*, *Mr. Holland's Opus*, etc.). Find your faith again so that you can walk back into your room and say out loud, "I believe in these learners," and mean it.

The power of your belief in your students is the cornerstone of change. Believe.

Interdependence

Difficult work builds community. This is why best friends are made in boot camp— where everyone is shocked, exhausted, and stuck with each other. Although I do not propose a yearlong mathematical boot camp, we can translate the design elements of boot camp—intensity, challenge, urgency, shared purpose—into the context of our math classes. Within the framework of challenging tasks, we can teach students the skills to successfully communicate, collaborate, and empathize with one another.

Task	Typical	Enriched
Opening	Students arrive in class, copy the problem from the board, complete the problem, and try to solve it. When time is up, teacher tells the right answer, and those who missed it change what they had written down.	Students work a problem. When time is up, teacher invites one student to share his work with all, then invites peers to ask questions, give feedback, and share alternate approaches.
Managing homework	Teacher projects correct answers on board, asks students to mark their own work, then turn in the corrected paper.	No answer key is provided. Students pair and share answers with one another. When they have different solutions, they compare their processes and discuss which solutions are correct and why.
Teacher presentation	Teacher introduces a new topic with a short lecture explaining the concept, gives definitions of necessary terms, demonstrates practice problems.	Minilesson: Teacher invites students to share and discuss what they already know about a topic, then links new information to their background knowledge by sharing new information; invites class to work demonstration problems collaboratively.
Work time	During work time, students complete tasks individually. Teacher answers students' questions and clarifies sources of confusion.	During work time, students may work alone or in small groups where all members contribute. Students needing help seek peers' assistance. Everyone is held accountable for thinking and learning.
End of class	Teacher tells class what they did and gives answers to any lingering questions.	Sharing and Reflection: Students talk about what they do and do not yet understand about the material. Learners respond to peers' questions. Teacher allows some questions to linger for further discussion.

Enhance typical tasks to promote collaboration.

Challenging tasks skillfully designed and facilitated not only promote student thinking but also require and promote collaboration. In the previous chapter, we discussed how one could enhance typical tasks to promote deeper understanding, which is often cultivated through collaborative learning experiences that surround these tasks.

Juicy learning experiences might include whole-group, small-group, or individual tasks, but it is the culture and expectation around those tasks that build the learning community and tighten the focus on student understanding. Let's take a look on the preceding page at some common classroom practices and consider how they could be enhanced to invite students as communities of learners to engage more deeply in the work of mathematical thinking.

Although these examples in the chart are only brief summaries of a few of the many possible approaches to adapting a workshop to enhance the classroom community of learners, you will notice that overall, the activities in the right-hand column put the responsibility for thinking and learning more squarely on the students' shoulders, and those experiences to the left rely more on the teacher to lead the way. When students are expected to engage fully in their learning community, they take ownership of the content, as well as the process, and thrive. In later chapters, these approaches will be fleshed out in greater detail.

Promote discourse.

In his article, "Never Say Anything a Kid Can Say!," teacher Steve Reinhart (2000) explains, "My definition of a good teacher has since changed from 'one who explains things so well that students understand' to 'one who gets students to explain things so well that they can be understood'" (54). In other words, he has shifted his role from that of explainer to that of coach, capitalizing on his students' ability to teach and learn from one another.

This leap to faith in students is a challenging one. We can conjure up so many reasons to doubt the role discourse might play with any particular group: What if they won't talk? What if they don't listen to each other? What if they get off task? What if they explain it wrong?

Discourse and community are symbiotic. In Chapter 5, we will look more specifically at structures that support academic discourse, but let us think first about how we can create a community that supports risk taking:

- Model curiosity. Among students, we can play the role of a learner as well, a learner learning about how others think. With the questions we ask and the inquisitiveness we demonstrate, we show by example what it means to be a member of a learning community: "Help me understand what you are thinking." "Tell me more."

- Model how to talk about ideas. Explicitly describe and teach the tone and vocabulary students need to share thinking. "I agree with Javier because. . . ." "Molly, can you explain more about. . . ." More ideas for these sorts of sentence stems are shared in Chapter 5.

- Demonstrate and expect respect for ideas. Learners may be in the habit of laughing at the mistakes of others, a tendency that may lead children to fall silent. We need to counter this with the edict that all ideas are good ideas, all questions are good questions, and all students have a right to change their minds. We can communicate this through words and actions, and most importantly, in our vigilance to stop a conversation and address any besmirching comment that crosses a child's lips.

- Teach empathy. Understanding how one's words and actions affect others is an important life lesson. We can teach empathy of this sort by talking about our and students' feelings and the ways that our comments can harm or hurt a peer's stamina and growth as a mathematician. We can read books, tell stories, and highlight classroom examples of empathy as they occur.

- Be willing to "press pause." What do you do when someone's opinion, idea, or feelings get thrown under the bus by another student's comment or attitude? If we press on, allowing that the other twenty-seven students in the room are still with us, we convey the message that an individual is not important. Instead, we need to be willing to put the brakes on academic progress and dedicate a moment to emotional intelligence: "How do you think Lydia feels right now? Why might she feel that way? What do we need to do to solve this problem?"

Scaffold successful collaborative learning.

Some students are unaccustomed to working together; others may have been permitted to do so poorly, or have gotten into bad habits.

I found that many of my entering seventh graders already despised group work, so at the start of each year we would take time to brainstorm all of the problems they had encountered in the past with shared tasks. These would typically include: someone takes over, someone does no work, someone loses the group's materials, we disagree on how to do the task, someone is absent, and so forth. Then, I would assign each table group a different problem to solve, and they would make a poster, for example: "What to do when someone takes over the group," listing

Figure 4.1 *One class' brainstorm on what it means to be a good group*

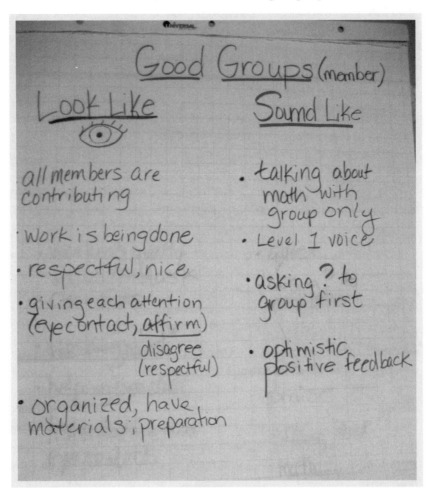

five to ten ideas to solve that problem. They would share their ideas with the whole group, discuss their nuances, add additional ideas, and then hang the chart in the classroom. Yes, this took two entire class periods, but then for the rest of the year, when someone came to me complaining about a group issue, I could refer him to these very helpful and practical charts.

Homeostasis

Just as all organisms in an ecosystem thrive when it is in perfect balance, or homeostasis, we can create similarly generative climates in our classrooms. We need strategies for keeping everyone in balance, even on the days when a sub comes in to cover.

Hold everyone accountable.

All the goodwill in the world may not inspire active participation by every learner every day. We need structures within our community that hold learners accountable for both academic participation and community-building contributions.

Before geometry teacher Ryan Martine staged a Socratic seminar inviting students to debate the value of the inclusive and exclusive definitions of trapezoids and kites, he required all students to read and annotate resources to build their background knowledge. The day of the event, those students who arrived without notes sat outside the circle of conversation, mute, and played a different role. Their job was to keep track of various data during the conversation: how many times each person spoke, the nature of their comments (for inclusive or exclusive definitions), as well as any questions asked. Although they still got to enjoy listening and learning as peers engaged in the discussion, they lost the privilege of full participation and had to spend that hour biting their tongues.

This artful instruction design invited two levels of accountability: All students were held accountable for arriving in class prepared to speak to the topic. Then, participation in the discussion was also tracked by the students outside the circle.

Though we may not enjoy frequent opportunities for Socratic seminars of this sort, we can learn from Ryan's example several elements of accountability:

- Individual preparation. Learners often succeed best in community endeavors when they have chances to read, write, and think alone for at least a few minutes before engaging with others. Create this preparation time to ensure that learners come to a group problem-solving task, a discussion, or a critique with thinking of their own to contribute.

- Entry and exit tickets. For students to gain participation in or move on from a task, require evidence of thinking (on paper or otherwise).

- Peer observations. Students can learn from observing and assessing the group. Create opportunities for learners to step out and monitor the classroom community, as well as the nature of individuals' comments. Teens can sometimes be the harshest critics of themselves and their colleagues, so we must be vigilant to temper their reports.

- Warm calling. Not modeled in the example above, there is another accountability strategy that I like to use called "warm calling." As opposed to "cold calling," which means randomly and suddenly calling on individuals, "warm calling" involves offering all learners time to think, write, and/or talk with peers about a topic before being randomly called upon to share their thinking. Warm calling demonstrates our expectation that every member is on track and participating, ready to share some ideas.

Offer authentic consequences.

Some transgressions of our community norms merit more than a bit of verbal feedback and call for consequences. As you levy these, think about restorative justice: What would assist the student in mending broken trust or an injured relationship? Oftentimes, learners themselves, when asked to do so, can develop appropriate means to make amends. ("So, the ruler is broken. What can you do to solve that problem?") Here are some community-affirming consequences to consider. A transgressor might:

- Write a letter of apology.

- Call her own parents to explain the problem.

- Help clean the classroom.

- Repair or replace a stolen or broken item, or work off the cost of its replacement.

- Sacrifice lunch, recess, or other free time to assist the teacher or community.

Alfie Kohn's books offer some great insight on classroom discipline, or for the less radical, I recommend reading up on the Love and Logic approach (Cline and Fay 2006). On the whole, I encourage you to devote far more time and energy to building community than to doling out consequences.

Give immediate feedback.

Throughout the flow of a workshop, we can target immediate, specific feedback to individuals and groups to channel their energy and efforts. For example, "Good job" is far flimsier than "Miguel, I appreciate how you are sticking with question four and trying to think about it in a new way after your first solution did not work out." A comment like this communicates to the entire community of learners the value that we place on stamina.

In addition to affirming students' positive participation, middle school math teacher Deb Maruyama does not pull punches when it comes to publically acknowledging those behaviors that detract from learners' progress.

"Why are you late? You are missing out on our learning time," she might say.

"Miss, you are calling me out in public!" the student retorts.

"You are late in public," she will explain, justifying that if a learner misbehaves in a public way, it is fair for a teacher to publically respond.

In addition to giving immediate verbal feedback to students as needed throughout a workshop, teachers can gather data about students' participation as a community during class time and present it as part of the reflection or closing at the end of the lesson. This could be done on the overhead or document camera, or just orally. Here are some structures to try:

- Notice/wonder: During class time, teacher records observations on a two-column chart—what he notices, what he wonders.

Notice	Matt's group finished the entire problem set, then went on to start their homework.
Wonder	Why was Tianna's group so quiet today?

- Rose and thorn: Teacher can note a rose and a thorn to individuals or groups—one thing they did well, one thing that was unfortunate.

  Rose: Elliot patiently explained his thinking to his group members, and Crystal asked good probing questions.

  Thorn: Max did not say much at all in the group conversation.

Facilitate self-monitoring.

Critical to students' future success is their ability to monitor and regulate their own behavior. As we begin a day's workshop or a unit's learning, we might choose a norm to focus on collectively or invite individuals to consider what might be a stretch goal for them in their participation as community members.

Then, we can create opportunities for learners to reflect in this way upon both their individual success at upholding our classroom community norms, as well as the ways in which their group members collectively lived up to those same norms.

This reflection could be invited in several ways:

- Silently. "Think about how well you took responsibility for your own learning today, and show me on a fist of five—five meaning you were amazing, three meaning you did okay, and zero showing that you blew it—how well you think you did."

- Small groups. "Get together in a group of three people who were not in your problem-solving group, and take thirty seconds each to talk about a way that you supported the learning of others today."

- Narrative form. "Write about the role you played in our learning community this week. Give specific examples of how you practiced two or more of our norms.

- Graphic organizer.

	Name the norm	Explain why
Norm I practiced effectively		
Norm I need to work on		

- Artistically. Sketch and label a picture of a time when you or another classmate was upholding one of our classroom norms.

- Appreciation circle. Circle up, and invite the group to acknowledge aloud classmates who demonstrated community-building behavior.

Though it may not be practical to reflect at length on a group's dynamics on a daily basis, frequent reference to and conversations about community norms ensure that we keep those alive over time, remaining vigilant to their importance in sustaining our learning community. More ideas on reflection are incorporated in Chapter 10.

Take your time. The community that exists in your classroom today did not evolve overnight, and a culture change requires perseverance and diligence. When considering the investment required to build community, we can remember the ethic of EMTs: "Go slow to go fast." As first responders come onto the scene of an accident, they assess the situation, gather data, and make a clear plan, lest they attend to a

Figure 4.2 *Student Reflection*

We would help other people in our table group until all were finished—we adopted the rule "No one is done until everyone in done." The greatest challenge in doing this project for me was helping and teaching the other people at my table. I had to work with them and help them understand and complete the graphs in the amount of time given. Even though at times it was hard and frustrating, I think it was good for me in the long run. Teaching somebody else how to do something helps me understand in depth why it works.

screaming patient with a broken arm without noticing the silent heart attack victim in the back seat. Similarly, as educators wanting to intentionally build culture, we need to slow down, plan our work, and work that plan. It is far more efficient to spend a whole period in August ensuring everyone understands the rationale behind your emphasis on classroom culture than to be called to answer the question "Why?" all year long. Be patient with your students, and with yourself.

"Yeah, but . . ."

"I have too much to cover, and no time to build community."

Community building does take time, yet it is time well spent: Once students feel safe and trusted in math class, they can relax and be honest about what they do and don't understand, share their thinking fearlessly, and support the growth of their peers. Cooperation and collaboration are life skills.

"I have students with special needs who are cognitively very low. How am I supposed to include them in a community?"

We need to believe in the assets of all learners and to model that asset stance before the whole group. Talk with the class about multiple intelligences and harnessing the abilities of peers. Remind students of the value of reciprocal teaching to deepen their own understanding. Differentiation will be addressed in greater detail in Chapter 8.

"What about kids who don't know English?"

Thinking can occur in any language. Allow English language learners to partner with same-language peers, if they have them, for some work but then invite students of various language backgrounds to collaborate also, encouraging them to share their thinking multimodally—in numbers, pictures, or other graphic representations. Academic language skills are enhanced by learners' participation in classroom discourse, as will be discussed in Chapter 5.

"This all sounds good, but you have not met Billy MacDuff. I just want him out of my class."

You are right; I have not yet met Billy MacDuff, but I have met thousands of children. In my experience, they all share a desire to be seen, to be appreciated, and to belong to a safe community that respects them for who they are. Look hard at Billy, and find that kernel of hope for him. Sincerely try some of the suggested strategies in the intention section of this chapter, talk to the people who love him, catch him doing something well, and see if even Billy MacDuff can find a home in your classroom and in your heart.

Quod Erat Demonstrandum

Making our classrooms safe spaces for all thinkers is a labor of love. Community can be established with strong intentions and intentionality, with opportunities for interdependent work and conversations, and with systems to maintain homeostasis. The process of building community requires significant investment of time and effort, yet the rewards of increased student engagement and deeper student understanding pay off. The work of building community is an affirmation of hope for humanity; if we can work together to make meaning of math, what else might be possible?

CHAPTER 5

Discourse

For most students, talk is the most important way of working on understanding. Talk is flexible; in talk, they can try out new ways of thinking and reshape an idea in mid-sentence, respond immediately to the hints and doubts of others, and collaborate in shaping meanings they could not hope to reach alone.

**—Douglas Barnes and Frankie Todd,
Communication and Learning Revisited**

Problem of the Day: Why ought and how can teachers facilitate learners' engagement in purposeful and meaningful conversations about their thinking?

Postulate: Students deepen their mathematical understanding by articulating their thinking, as well as responding to the ideas of others, during intentional classroom conversations.

I remember getting to talk a lot in math class as a kid: My teacher would stand at the board and lead us through an exercise that sounded something like this, "So, we have $3x - 5 = 16$, and we need to solve for x, so we need to get x by itself. What is the first thing I do?"

"Add five to both sides!" a bunch of us would yell out, and she would mash her chalk against the board and do just that.

"Now, those fives cancel, and we have $3x = 16 + 5$. What is $16 + 5$?"

"Twenty-one!" we hollered.

"Good! Twenty-one." She would write, "$3x = 21$," then ask, "What do I do next?"

"Divide both sides by three!"

"Okay, $3x \div 3$ is?"

"x!"

"And, $21 \div 3$ is?"

"Seven!"

"So, $x =$?"

"Seven."

"Good!"

Sound familiar? What fun. Even though we were in algebra class, all we had to do was perform arithmetic one step at a time, and the teacher would do the rest. She did most of the thinking for us. This typical teacher-initiated QRE—question, response, evaluation—pattern is not the sort of classroom discourse that cultivates understanding. Instead, discourse involves learners making meaning of content through accountable, engaged conversations about their thinking in small or large groups.

In this chapter we will discuss the value of high-quality discourse, and the means to scaffold it in a learning community.

School Today

In contrast to my days as a student seated in straight rows facing front while the teacher stood at the board leading the class, students today are often seated in table groups or invited to cluster their desks together to work. Surely, one would hope, this modern arrangement would promote more active academic conversations.

Just out of curiosity, I conducted an informal research project: For several days observing math classes in a local middle school, I tracked the kinds of talk audible among students during math class work time; here is what I heard (in order of frequency):

- gossip

  "Did you hear that Giovanni dumped Lissette?"

  "No way! Is that why she was crying in the bathroom?"

- playing

  "Here! Throw it!"

- teasing

  "Why you wearin' that Broncos' jersey, man? Don't you know they lost yesterday?"

- social plans

  "Jamie and I are going to the mall Friday after school; want to meet us?"

  "Can't. Have practice, but maybe after. How late will you be there?"

- tattling

  "Miss! She's texting!"

- complaining

  "I hate this class."

  "Me too. She gives way too much homework."

- negotiating for answers/materials

  "Gimme the answer to number five."

  "No way."

  "Come on. I already got six. I'll give that one to you."

- put-downs

  "You stupid?"

- directing

  "Take out your book! She said take out your book!"

Students made all of the comments above—and many more like them—during learning time, time when they had some sort of math work in front of them. Once in a while, I did hear peers assisting one another with the problems at hand, but that kind of conversation made up less than 10 percent of what happened to be audible on those days at that particular school.

After listening to the student sound track, I shifted my attention to teacher talk for a few days. In addition to offering direct instruction, I wondered, in what ways are teachers addressing students? In order of frequency, I heard adults policing, socializing, directing, praising, correcting, accounting, and rescuing. Teacher talk will be discussed further in Chapter 9.

Through my research, I grew convinced that this is what typical school tends to sound like to students: adults policing, praising, and directing while students gossip, play, and tease. These modes of communication only serve to reinforce the power structures of traditional schools: teachers as "bosses" and students as "workers" looking to avoid both punishment and toil to the greatest extent possible. How can we engage students in conversations that invite them to take ownership of their own thinking, as well as to grow curious about the ideas of others?

Why Discourse?

Generative discourse is intentional, focused, accountable conversation about ideas, and it is contagious. When students are engaged as learners, sharing, discussing, and evaluating one another's thinking in a mutually supportive setting, they are constructing their own understanding of the concepts at hand. Discourse permeates a minds-on math workshop; the minilesson, work time, and sharing and reflection are all wonderful forums for students to talk about their thinking and to respond to the thinking of peers.

Discourse can be challenging to establish and facilitate, yet the rewards of establishing norms and habits of productive student discourse are well worth the investment. Discourse

- engages learners
- promotes understanding
- develops communication and collaboration skills
- supports academic language development.

Discourse engages learners.

A teenager once described his school experience to me as a process of shuffling: shuffling papers, shuffling from room to room. Of 171,000 students in twenty-six states surveyed in 2005, less than a third reported feeling excited about their classes (High School Survey of Student Engagement quoted in Quate and McDermott 2010, 6). Yet, we know that for learning to take place, students need to be drawn into the learning process.

> Learning and succeeding in school requires active engagement—
> whether students are rich or poor, black, brown, or white. The
> core principles that underlie engagement are applicable to
> all students—whether they are in urban, suburban, or rural
> communities. (National Research Council 2004, 1)

Students are social animals. When we invite learners to engage in classroom discourse, we harness their innate desire to communicate with peers and put that desire to work in service of learning. Well-designed discourse can engage even the most reluctant by communicating to them the great value we place on their ideas.

Discourse promotes understanding.

"Oh! Now I get it!" Have you ever heard such exclamations as students talked through their work with peers? Often, classmates can readily empathize with points of confusion more than we seasoned teachers who have been seeing the same math for years; learners can explain ideas in terms more accessible to students in the group, yet too often we teachers feel that we can explain things "best." Yet, research points to the power of reciprocal teaching in enhancing the learning not only of the listener, but also of the student who works to explain. Discourse welcomes multiple approaches to modeling a concept or solution, while driving at the shared goal of understanding.

To understand content well, students need opportunities to wrestle with ideas, test theories, defend positions, and to get inside a conjecture and work to match it up with the world. Focused academic conversations provide a key opportunity for these sorts of mental gymnastics. "As Socrates well understood, learning is more likely to change through dialogue and reflection than through lecture and imposition" (Kober 1993, 44). Discourse is that dialogue.

Discourse develops communication and collaboration skills.

Tony Wagner justifies his push for schools to focus on twenty-first-century skills: "In order to get good jobs, and to be active and informed citizens in our democracy, economy, today's students—and tomorrow's workers—need to learn how to . . . work in teams and lead by influence, be agile and adaptable, communicate clearly and concisely" (Wagner 2008, 339). The Common Core promotes this sort of agility and multifaceted literacy across the curriculum, and classroom discourse in math creates multiple opportunities to practice communication and collaboration, creativity and innovation, critical thinking and problem solving.

Discourse supports academic language development.

Immigration brings students from all over the world together to learn in many of our schools. Between 1995 and 2005, seven states saw a 300 percent increase in the number of English language learners enrolled in public schools. For culturally and linguistically diverse students to succeed as scholars, they must not only hone their ability to communicate in conversational English, but also practice using the academic language of the content areas. As research on language acquisition informs us, "Language development is an active, not passive process. Teachers must give students opportunities and time to talk, which means teachers must make key shifts: talk less, listen more" (Klaus-Quinlan and Nathansen-Mejia 2010, 16). Herein is another reason to shape and scaffold rich, deep, meaningful opportunities for learners to engage with one another as mathematicians.

Creating and Sustaining Effective Discourse

Let's listen in again to another excerpt from the classroom of Rachel Rosenberg, fourth-grade teacher at Denver's Harrington Elementary. As you read, you may begin to wonder, "How did she get those kids to talk like that?" which is exactly what we are going to discuss next.

Ms. Rosenberg: Let's just do a quick number of the day. Let's take a minute to activate prior knowledge. What properties of the number three are important? What's important about that number? Who would like to open up our conversation? Martin has something. . . . Anabelle, I'll be coming to you.

Edgar: It's an odd number.

Luisa: It has factors.

Ms. Rosenberg: We're connecting to Edgar. Do you agree, disagree?

Luisa: I agree that it's an odd number because it's one more than two.

Clarissa: It's an odd number because. . . .

Ms. Rosenberg: So you're agreeing with Luisa? Because she just said that. What do we know about all odd numbers?

Arturo: It's odd because two, four. . . .

Ms. Rosenberg: What's that called, when you're skip-counting by a number?

Salvador: Multiplication.

Ms. Rosenberg: It's like that, because that's how you multiply. It's a multiple. I love that way of explaining that it's odd, because when you skip-count by twos, you don't land on three.

Salvador: Prime number.

Ms. Rosenberg: Do you agree or disagree?

Maricela: I agree with Clarissa because it's like the odd number.

Ms. Rosenberg: So all odd numbers are prime?

Maricela: No . . . like nine.

Ms. Rosenberg: So nine is a prime number? Do you guys agree? Anabelle, is nine a prime number?

Maricela: I disagree with myself because $3 \times 3 = 9$.

Ms. Rosenberg: So, is that a prime?

Salvador: It's a composite.

David: I have a wondering. What if it's not a prime or a composite?

Ms. Rosenberg: That's a great question. We'll have to look at the definitions to see if there are numbers that don't fit into either.

Martin: I have a question about skip-counting. Can you skip-count by every number, like zero, one, two?

Ms. Rosenberg: Let's try skip-counting by zero. Zero, zero. I love that question, so Martin, be sure to write that down.

This very brief excerpt illustrates many key features of classroom discourse: the shift in the role of the teacher from expert to facilitator, and the shift in the voices of the students, from answer providers ("Seven!" my classmates and I shouted out in my seventh-grade math class) to explainers of thinking. These are fourth graders, primarily English language learners, and every day Rachel gets them thinking and reasoning as mathematicians. She works hard to scaffold discourse in her classroom, knowing that the skills of communicating about ideas are critical to children's success and esteem. She is aware of how her tone and comments shape the classroom culture, and she explicitly teaches and regularly reinforces the conversational and thinking skills students need in academic conversations.

As the lead learners in our minds-on math workshops, our stance has significant power in influencing the attitudes of students toward their own thinking and that of their peers. Let us examine some critical teacher moves one at a time, as they may be employed in the context of any discourse structure, whether brief paired sharing, small-group work, or whole-class discussion. The constellation of questions that follows is by no means a daily prescription, but rather a menu of choices from which you might choose one or more on a regular basis as you cultivate discourse within your community of learners.

Create an atmosphere of respect for thinking.

For students to do the brave work of sharing their thinking and sometimes publicly disagreeing with themselves, learners need to feel safe in our classrooms. This safety is a hard-won culture created by deliberate effort over time.

Respect for thinking is more than just a rule ("No put-downs"). We model respect for the thinking of our students in the way we regard their efforts and celebrate their mental flexibility. We do this in the ways that we invite and respond to the thinking of students, whether talking with them as individuals, small groups, or the entire class. To this end, we may:

- express curiosity ("I am so curious about how you will solve for *x*.")

- request assistance ("Help me to understand why you decided to graph those equations first.")

- applaud courage ("Neisa is modeling courage by sharing her thinking with the whole group.")

- welcome diversity ("Wow! You are showing us a new way of understanding the graph.")

- voice gratitude ("Thank you for sharing that interesting idea with us.").

As Suzanne Chapin encourages in *Classroom Discussions* (2003), we can invite students to perceive incorrect answers as stepping-stones along the road to understanding, rather than embarrassing mistakes to be covered up. We can model the language of disagreeing with one's self rather than feeling "wrong." We can consistently laud students for the progress they are making and helping one another to make. We can welcome alternate approaches rather than stopping after one "right" answer is presented. And we can encourage and warmly welcome all contributions, especially those from reluctant learners.

Part of showing respect for thinking is making the time that thinking needs. We must let there be windows of silence within conversation to allow time for learners to ponder ideas—theirs and their peers'. Resist the temptation to immediately call on the first person who raises her hand and instead silently count to ten in your head after posing a question to promote thinking by all.

Ask learners to share their problem-solving processes.

Brilliant as we may be at demonstrating and explaining the intricacies of mathematical ideas, there comes a time—earlier than we think—in each learning sequence when we must relinquish the mic and invite students to tell what they know and understand in their own ways. Inviting students to explain takes patience and time. Initially, they may try to escape the spotlight with as few words as possible, but with careful modeling and coaching, they will increase their confidence and competence at describing what they know and understand.

Inviting students to explain to their peers is more than simply borrowing a child's paper and flashing it under the document camera to illustrate a correct answer. For learners to explain their own solutions, we need to physically and verbally get out of the way: move away from the front of the room, listen more than you talk, interject only as needed to prompt further verbalization, let the student presenter have the floor, and be patient.

We can encourage a student (speaking either to you individually, to a partner or small group, or to the whole class) by inviting them to:

- describe their process ("How did you start? Talk through your thinking.")

- reflect on their decisions ("What were some of the decisions you made as a problem solver?")

- explain their vigilance ("What were some of the speed bumps you encountered when solving this problem?")

- confirm their thinking ("How do you know you are right?")

- make connections ("What is the big idea of this problem, and how could you apply this concept to other problems?")

- promote discourse ("What kind of feedback would you like from me/the group?").

Invite peers' comments and questions.

As we remove ourselves from center stage as presenters, we can also relinquish the role of critic. Students can competently critique their peers' work and thinking, revealing more about their own understanding and misconceptions than sitting and listening to us perhaps ever could.

Considerate critique is a learned skill, one we can explicitly teach by taking the time to discuss what sorts of comments are helpful, hurtful, or bland. Through description, modeling, practice, observation, and reflection, students can learn to speak kindly and thoughtfully to one another. Slow the conversation down; be willing to stop after a student speaks and to discuss whether his words were respectful and constructive and to be honest with individuals whose words detract from the learning community. We need to make a deliberate commitment to halt any trains of conversation that undermine the fabric of our community.

Also, we can guide students to be specific in their speech. Too often, I visit classrooms where a student shares a beautiful explanation, then a hovering teacher hops in with, "Very good!" "Exactly right!" or some other seemingly affirming comment, short-circuiting any discussion. Although the learner may very well be exactly correct in her work, by seizing the opportunity to announce this to the group, we thwart the audience's thinking. When instead we invite students to voice what *they* think of this peer's work, we promote leadership and ownership of the learning in our class.

How can we invite peers' to reflect on a student's sharing?

- Propose reflection ("What do you think about Joanna's work?").

- Promote questioning ("What questions do you have for Joanna?").

- Invite comparison ("How does Joanna's thinking compare with your thinking?").

If the conversation slows, we may try to:

- check for agreement ("Did everyone get the same solution that Joanna got/ do what Joanna did?")

- encourage divergent thinking ("Are there other ways to think about this?").

Remember that there are many ways to get to a correct answer; encourage alternate approaches and discussion of which tack is most effective for a particular problem.

Thinking on your feet is a challenge! Many students benefit from "think time" before being asked to speak. Whether it is a moment of silent reflection or an opportunity to write before a conversation, or simply a pause mid-discussion to invite learners to synthesize what they are hearing and gather their thoughts, research shows that when we allow for silence and thinking, students are more likely to form complete sentences and to comment specifically on the ideas of others in the group. Silence promotes discourse.

In addition to asking good questions and opening the floor to student voices, we need to explicitly teach students how to talk about their ideas with the group. Learners often appreciate the support of sentence stems to help them articulate their thinking. Here are some to try.

Explaining their own thinking, students might try:

- I think . . . because . . .

- When I first saw this problem, I thought . . .

- This reminds me of . . .

- I would like to know . . .

- I used to think . . . and now I think . . .

TYPICAL SHARING VS. MINDS-ON DISCOURSE

	Typical sharing	**Minds-on discourse**
Positions	Teacher remains at front of room. Student presenter may share from desk, give teacher her paper, or come to front.	Student presenter stands at front of group while teacher steps to the side.
Content	Student shows or shares an answer.	Student explains how he approached the problem and why he believes his solution is accurate.
Response	Teacher verifies accuracy of student's answer or corrects any errors.	Classmates respond with questions and feedback, compare their ideas to those of the presenter, share alternate approaches.

Again how do you get 1st graders to do this?

In responding to the ideas of others, students could start with:

- I agree with . . . because . . .
- I disagree with . . . because . . .
- I am wondering . . .
- How did you know to . . .
- Can you explain . . .

Practice using these in conversations about simple things—what the tadpole in the fish tank is doing, what is happening outside the classroom window. Post the stems you like on a wall so students can refer to them. Learners also begin to mimic the questions and comments of their teachers, so in addition to introducing and practicing sentence stems like these, you can demonstrate by your own example every day what it looks and sounds like to be a part of a community of thinkers engaged in academic discourse.

Take time to uncover errors.

Tempting as it may be to stop the conversation once a correct answer has been established, investing in further discussion about a problem's alternate—and even incorrect—solutions will greatly benefit the very learners who made those errors, as well as their peers, as described in the helpful article, "What's Right About Looking at What's Wrong?" (Schifter 2007). Creating time and space to shine light on, dissect, and analyze errors leads all to a deeper understanding of the problems' pitfalls and how one might better avoid them in similar problems in the future. Frame mistakes as opportunities to investigate further; compliment those willing to share their thinking, whether correct or otherwise.

We might encourage this reflection by inviting learners to

- share multiple solutions ("What other answers did folks get?")
- pinpoint decisions ("What were the critical decision points in solving this problem?")
- assess errors' impact ("How would a wrong turn affect your work?")
- categorize mistakes ("What kinds of errors made you stumble?")
- identify signposts ("Were there any clues that you might have missed along the way?")
- generalize ("What do we need to remember in order to solve problems like these accurately?").

Let students revise their own thinking.

Metacognition—thinking about one's own thinking—is integral to the learning process. When we monitor for meaning, notice when we comprehend and when we don't, and work to make sense of a puzzling situation, we are actively engaging our minds in the work of understanding. This process of understanding is so important, it comes first in the Common Core Standards for Mathematical Practice: Make sense of problems and persevere in solving them. For math learners, this minds-on approach is essential, yet far too often overlooked.

When we allow students to unearth the truth about inaccurate thinking in a safe atmosphere, we free them from the looming progression of thoughts: "I was wrong, I don't get it, and I hate math." An incorrect answer is the beginning of learning: when we maximize the opportunities revealed by our own and our students' mistakes, we model the growth mindset, the belief that we are all capable of overcoming our difficulties and achieving.

We can take inspiration from Winston Churchill's famous and brief commencement speech, "Never, never, never, never give up." Getting a wrong answer, even through great effort, is not defeat. Defeat lies in stopping at that answer, accepting it as simply incorrect rather than striving to understand one's own mistake and the learning opportunity it presents. Victory lies in unveiling errors and courageously finding one's way through to comprehension.

We can invite students to revise their thinking by asking them to:

- synthesize ("Do you still agree with your earlier thinking?")

- observe growth ("How has your thinking changed?")

- extract learning ("What's the lesson of this problem?")

- reflect on their strengths and challenges ("What did you learn about yourself as a mathematician today?").

Scaffolding Discourse

Within a community of learners, with a teacher cultivating the dispositions described above, discourse can take many forms. Given specific conversation formats, modeling, clear accountability, opportunities for reflection, and systems for assessment, students can capitalize on opportunities to hone their mathematical thinking through conversations with peers.

Conversation Formats for Sharing Mathematical Thinking

There is a great abundance of conversation structures, many of which you have probably experienced or utilized. Here are a few quick and easy structures that can be rehearsed and integrated into a math class at regular intervals. For each, I offer some sentence starters that students could practice using. For any new structure we introduce to students, it is well worth the time to present and explain the structure, rehearse it around a fairly easy topic, ease into the math content, and then invite students to practice, observe one another, and reflect on their effective use of the structure. To implement these structures

---

What do you do when a student says, "I don't know"?

It might only take drawing two popsicle sticks drawn from your jar, reading the students' names on each before you come across one who answers with the too often heard refrain, "I don't know." What we do when a student says, "IDK," or otherwise shrugs off the invitation to participate in our learning community is critical: We must be relentless. It is okay not to know, but it is not okay not to *try* to know. So, how do I respond?

Psychologist: "Well, if you *did* know, what do you think you might say?"

Zen: "We have plenty of time to wait until you are ready to share your thinking."

Who Wants to Be a Millionaire: "Would you like to phone a friend?"

Love and Logic: "We are really hopeful that you will share your ideas now, rather than need to come in at lunch to write a letter to the class about this topic."

You probably have other tricks up your sleeve, but "IDK" is really a test of our convictions, an opportunity for us to convey our beliefs about students to them: If we let Josie off the hook this time, what message does that send to her and the rest of the class about our expectations? If we believe, as does Dr. Carol Dweck, in the growth mindset, we must read "IDK" as a teachable moment, an opportunity to reinforce our expectations that students can and will understand, not allow them to languish in the fixed mindset where they believe they don't and can't get it.

Structure	Description	Sentence Starters
Pair and share	Students turn to a neighbor and briefly share their own thinking, then listen to the thinking of their partner.	"I am thinking . . . because . . ." "I had a different idea. I was thinking . . . because . . ."
Problem discussion	In small groups, students work together to solve a problem.	"I think we should . . . because . . ." "I disagree with . . . because . . ." "What if we . . ."
Carousel discussion	In small groups, students either respond to written information or gather thinking about a topic by writing on a shared piece of paper; the paper is then passed on to the next group.	"What do you think about . . ." "I am wondering . . ." "I don't understand . . ." "One question I have is . . ."
Peer critique	One student comes to the board and presents her work or thinking about a certain problem to the whole class; peers observe and then respond with comments, questions, and comparisons.	After presenter explains, peers may say, "I like how you . . ." "Can you help me understand . . ." "Why did you . . ."

successfully, teachers need to explicitly name what students should be doing and notice when their conversations do or do not meet the expectations.

What many experienced teachers find is that no conversation format alone is sufficient to ensure discourse, but that when we add modeling, accountability, reflection, and assessment, students are more likely to engage in ways that deepen their understanding of the content at hand. Let's look at each of these integral processes in turn.

✱ be more explicit with turn and talk ✱

Modeling

Before asking students to "turn and talk," we need to be explicit about the content of the conversations we anticipate hearing. In the early days, our students may need sentence stems and other cues to kick off their interchange. Not only do we need to explain these orally, but also demonstrate them to the whole class by actively presenting a small skit of a quality conversation.

"Okay, I need a couple of volunteers up here. Raul, Vince. Thanks," the teacher calls two students to the front, and offers them each a chair. *"So, when I say turn and talk, this is what I mean,"* she continues. *"You are going to turn to the person sitting next to you—not across the aisle—not behind you, the person sharing your table, so let's not waste time looking for different partners. You are going to turn to the partner at your table and talk with them about the topic or question. Let's practice with something easy."* She puts her hands on the boys' shoulders, *"Guys, I'd like you to turn and talk about what you had for lunch."* A snicker rumbles through the room, but the boys up front are willing to play along.

"Uh, what'd you have?" Raul asks.

"Chili dog and chips. You?"

"Same, without the chili."

"So, just a plain hot dog?"

"Yah, with ketchup."

"Cool." Vince looks back to his teacher with a bit of a shrug.

"Exactly! Brilliant!" she affirms. *"So,"* she turns to the class, *"What did you just see them do?"*

"They asked each other to share."

"They listened to each other's answers."

"They both got turns to talk."

"Vince asked a question to find out whether his hot dog was plain."

"Eye contact."

"Right on! You guys all already know how to do this, have a conversation, so now, I am just asking you to apply those same conversation skills to your math learning. A turn and talk is quick, easy, but focused on the question, and then over. Ready to try it?" She asks students next to turn and talk about their math learning: What do conic sections have to do with parabolas?

After a few minutes of turning and talking, the teacher calls the group back together and gathers students' ideas about the question. Then, she asks them to turn and talk again with the same partner, this time about how well they felt they did with the first task. *"What went well in your turn and talk? What could have made it even better?"* This opportunity

for reflection and self-evaluation is a critical step in developing students'
abilities to independently engage in the learning behaviors we rehearse.

Turn and talk is but one small, simple example of a conversation structure that, like all others, initially must be supported with clear instructions and demonstration and followed up with distinct feedback. Otherwise, those three minutes in our lesson plan that we designated for promoting discourse and building community can become time wasted.

So, just as we must teach students math content through explicit instruction and carefully designed experiences, so also we need to instruct students about the behaviors that promote academic discourse. These are life lessons.

Accountability

Now I don't know if this has ever happened to you, but the first time I modeled and then asked students to turn and talk about their mathematical thinking, they quickly commenced a discussion about Halloween costumes . . . so frustrating. But the truth is, much as we would love to think that learners will all be so riveted by the opportunity to discuss the relationship between complementary and supplementary angles that nothing else might cross their young minds, few students may feel inclined to stay on topic unless they are aware of some extrinsic accountability systems. There are a lot you could choose from; the following are some of my favorites.

Teaching Others As noted by John Hattie in *Visible Learning* (2009), reciprocal teaching is one of the most effective means of deepening students' understanding. It is also an exquisite way to hold learners accountable for discourse and other tasks. Essentially, we are saying to them, "The whole group is relying on you to develop expertise in this area, so please be responsible!" There are many ways to create opportunities for teaching others:

- Jigsaw: A jigsaw essentially has two parts: First, students become experts; then, those experts teach others from their expertise. Let's say you are studying data displays. In the first round, you might assign each expert group a different one to study: circle graph, box and whisker plot, histogram, line graph, and so forth. Then after time to master their particular data display, expert group members separate and join learning groups: a group with one expert on each data display ready to teach peers.

- Museum sharing: This is another great format to ensure more students are thinking and talking more of the time during sharing. It was invented by my colleague, science teacher Jeff Cazier. Here is how he sets it up: Let's say students worked in teams of three during work time. In each team of three, students decide who is person A, B, and C. At the end of work time, Jeff does three rounds of sharing. Each person presents their own group's work once, then for the other two rounds visits and learns from other presenters.

The first round is just two minutes. The A partners stay at their original table. The B and C partners from every group circulate to listen to other A presenters. Students who are circulating are encouraged to record their learning in writing while they listen to peers. In round two, the B partners return to their original tables and become the presenter. The A and C partners circulate. In round three, the Cs present. As and Bs circulate. In this way, each learner, alone, must speak to peers about what his group discussed and discovered.

- Presentations: Students master a skill or create a product, then teach it or share it before the whole class. Along with traditional student posters and displays, here are some other formats students could use to share their original thinking: blogs, children's book, comic strip, diorama, film, foldable, mobile, model, placemat, podcast, poem, poster, proof, slide show, song, speech, wiki . . . the possibilities are endless.

All of these presentation formats engage audiences best when all learners have a job as they listen to their peers—some accountability for listening, asking questions, taking notes, then doing something to synthesize those, whether as a Venn diagram, mind map, or narrative summary.

Observations As a science teacher, I sometimes leaned back and envisioned my classroom as a large petri dish where I did experiments on the young learners in my midst: I would try new structures and strategies, then observe their responses. I would sometimes document and share those observations with students, with names attached. One structure for doing so I learned from master literacy teacher Cris Tovani: while her students are working, she grabs a clipboard and lays out three columns on a sheet of paper: (+) for noting things students are doing well that contribute to their learning and that of the group, (" ") for thoughtful and interesting comments, and (−) for unfortunate behaviors.

+	" "	−
When Shira was confused, Jose used a graph to show how he got his answer.	"Cool! Now, I get it!"—Shaunique "Help me understand."—Beth	Evan spilled the markers but did not help pick them up.

This sort of data can be flashed up on the SMART Board or shared on the document camera to spark conversation about the ways in which the students' discourse contributed to their mathematical understanding on a given day. Refer to the other ideas for feedback in Chapter 4, and think about how to best remind your students of your high hopes for them as thinkers and learners, a community.

Reporting Out As a teacher, I am of the mind that when I offer learners opportunities to think, talk, or write about something during class, I am then free to call upon whomever I like to share their thinking. Although distinct from cold calling—randomly calling on students without offering them time to prepare—this style of "warm calling" lets students know that they will have time to warm up, think about a question, but that during that time, they need to be focused and responsible because they might be the lucky one who gets to offer her thinking to the group.

Access Another accountability structure we might employ is that of access: Whoever makes wise choices to participate positively in classroom discourse earns a privilege, whether a sticker or a snack or a chance at the board or a turn on the classroom computer, or . . . you name it. Although some folks think offering students privileges for doing what they were supposed to do anyhow is counter to the goal of them developing intrinsic motivation, the truth is we all love to be rewarded from time to time.

Reflection

Students appreciate the value of discourse when they see the ways in which listening to peers' thinking and sharing their own deepen their grasp of the content. As with all other skills we strive to teach, it is useful to stop at regular intervals and reflect, "How is this working for you? What are you learning about yourself as a math learner through this process?" Reflection will be discussed more in Chapter 10.

"Yeah, but . . ."

"Discussing every problem is really time-consuming!"

Research shows that students benefit more from solving and then discussing a few problems in depth, rather than completing numerous practice problems. When we choose the featured problem for our discussion carefully, we can reveal a great deal of conceptual understanding and uncover a number of potential mathematical hazards, assess students' comprehension, and build their confidence. What better use of time in our math classes?

"My students only listen to me."

Unfortunately, too often students attend only to the teacher's voice, disregarding the academic understanding of their peers. When we allow ourselves alone to be the presenters and assessors in our classrooms, we suggest to learners that they themselves are not capable of the sort of thinking and reasoning that understanding and explaining mathematics require. No, we must insist that all can and should be respected to share their ideas and that learners listen to the thoughts of peers and then all use the logic of their own good minds to assess the accuracy of the solutions of their colleagues. Let the learners do the work.

"All this discussion just confuses students. They want me to tell them the right answer."

Teacher Steven C. Reinhart describes his role in promoting thinking in "Never Say Anything a Kid Can Say!":

> "Is this the right answer?" Students frequently ask this question. My usual response to this question might be that "I'm not sure. Can you explain your thinking to me?" As soon as I tell students that the answer is correct, thinking stops. (2000, 56)

Minds-on math workshops are about thinking.

Quod Erat Demonstrandum

Discourse is challenging to orchestrate and facilitate yet one of the most important life and learning skills we can impart. To become effective in our role promoting classroom discourse, we need to give time to conversations, relinquish control over the flow of ideas, and train students in the patterns of conversation that promote sharing of thinking. Students master discourse when we offer them structures, model and practice skills, then reflect upon our collective efficacy as a community of thinkers.

CHAPTER 6

Opening

Without rich opportunities to develop one's ability to sharpen awareness and to enhance an inclination and motivation for thinking, it is difficult to get smarter.

—**Ron Ritchhart, Intellectual Character**

Problem of the Day: How do you start math class?

Postulate: The launch pad for an effective math workshop is a crisp opening that welcomes learners, invites them to connect to their own background knowledge, and sets purpose for learning.

I was cleaning out my basement the other day and came across an interesting artifact: an entire box full of overhead transparencies (remember those?) from one of my first years teaching middle school math. Each one is a different "Problem of the Day"—math problems I used to ask students to do at the very beginning of class every day. But then, on each transparency, telltale evidence of my folly has stood the test of time: Below each question is an illustrated explanation of the solution—*in my handwriting.* When I saw this, I had a terrible flashback. Here was my opening routine those first years in the classroom:

Students would enter, take out their math notebooks (composition books), copy down the problem, then solve it. Sound okay? But here's the thing: Most would just write down the problem and stop. They knew that if they waited long enough, I would go ahead and explain the right answer on the overhead, and they could just copy that down. When I collected their notebooks, I had no way of knowing whether the answer represented their thinking, or merely replicated mine.

It was not until my first coach observed me teaching math and took note of this unfortunate routine that I began to change my ways. "What do you want them to be thinking about in those first few minutes of class?" she asked me.

I had an answer, "How smart they are, how they know this stuff already." I waved my hand at the then-growing stack of transparencies on my overhead cart.

"But look at what they are doing," she sweetly pointed out. "They copy, then wait, then copy some more. What's the lesson there?"

"Math is about copying, being patient, and copying."

"And so how is this opening serving your purpose?"

I had to think of another way.

Starting the class with a math task is a great way to engage learners and get them thinking right away—if we set it up so that this is actually what happens. As a young teacher, I held the conviction that all learners are capable of brilliance, and I wanted them to begin class by experiencing their own strength, but my practice, as described above, was not effectively creating that opportunity.

If we want to start our math learning time by signaling to students our confidence in their capabilities, we need to ask them not only to put their good minds to work promptly, but also to hold them accountable for working well, then to kindle their curiosity about the learning before them. We do this by devoting the first few minutes of class to an opening routine that invites learners to make connections and establish purpose.

Remember that in a minds-on math workshop, the opening precedes and differs in intention from the minilesson, though they can often blend together. The opening is the warm-up, the hook. The minilesson is the portion of the workshop where we offer a small dose of direct instruction, model thinking, and prepare students for independent work.

In this chapter, we will explore four aspects of an effective opening routine:

- welcoming learners
- students activating prior knowledge related to the day's work
- learners setting purpose for this lesson
- managing homework.

In this chapter, you will read about a variety of strategies to these four ends. On any given day, your opening may only address one, two, or three of these, yet the objective remains: Use those first five minutes of class to motivate and engage learners. Here are some effective approaches you might assemble into a daily routine that will serve as a springboard into your minilesson.

Welcoming Learners

What does it feel like to walk into your classroom? What do learners see? What kinds of things are you saying to students as they enter? How are they beginning their work as mathematicians? Those first ninety seconds, even before the bell rings, are a key opportunity to convey our beliefs about learners and our learning community: You are capable mathematicians, and we are here together to do good, hard work. If you are working in a self-contained classroom, your transition to math time can signal enthusiasm and confidence—a math-related song, a quick fun quiz game, a moment of reflection on what it means to have stamina as a mathematician. You are readying your team for game seven of the World Series, and you need them in top mental form.

Whenever learners are entering, avoid catching up on email and paperwork, and instead spend those first minutes attending to the needs and dispositions of students. Here are some quick and easy tone setters most teachers already know, but sometimes forget amid the pressures of school:

- Meet learners at the door.
- Greet learners by name.
- Ask individuals how they are doing, and mean it.
- Give authentic compliments.
- Smile.

When we start the class with energy, intention, and optimism, we uphold and promote community.

Students Activating Prior Knowledge with an Opening Exercise

As we know from the work of the National Research Council (2005), students learn best when we start a lesson by creating an opportunity for them to activate their background knowledge.

An opening problem or question is a useful structure for inviting learners to reflect on what they already know about a topic, and as well as to allow them to air what Merseth (1993) called "naïve theories"—preconceived, perhaps inaccurate notions about the nature of a concept. When we explicitly and intentionally explore students' background knowledge, we put all ideas on the table so that through the course of the learning experience any areas of confusion may see the light of day.

Whether they call it the "Day Starter," "Do Now," "Math Message," "Problem of the Day," or "Warm-Up," many math teachers open class with an exercise of some sort designed to get everyone in their seats and started on some mathematical thinking. This is a wonderful opportunity to activate prior knowledge related to the day's work! A strong, independent, well-designed, and thoughtfully facilitated Day Starter that begins at the bell sends learners important messages:

- You know what to do.

- You are here to work.

- You are capable of individual success as a mathematician.

Let's start by looking at the nature of the opening problem, then look at how we can build a routine that supports thoughtful engagement by all learners.

Setting Up Success

If we want students to use those first five minutes of class to engage in some mathematical thinking, we need to support all learners' success as well as hold them accountable for effort. Some students shut down as soon as they see a math question on the board and prefer to hide out, hunch over, and jot some fake math on their papers, or maybe just wait us out. We can reverse this tendency by offering learners opening tasks that are open ended, with a foothold for everyone. In addition, we need to build some accountability motivating each student to engage with those tasks.

Consider the virtues of starting class by asking accessible questions, rather than quiz problems: Everyone can get started; everyone can experience some success; you can still gather useful formative assessment data.

Figure 6.1a *Day Starter*

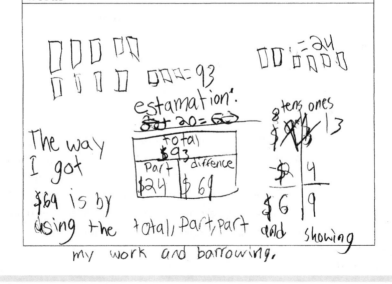

Problem number 2

Part A

Zaynie is saving money to buy a new Star Wars Lego set. He has saved $93. Last night at the museum, he showed no self-control, and spent $24 on a dinosaur fossil kit. How much money does Zaynie have left after last night's purchase? — *means buy*

Background Knowledge: What do I already know that will help me solve the problem?

I know that Zaynie had $93 and spent $24 for a dinosaur fossil kit.

Solve the problem using pictures, numbers and or words

□□□ □□
□ □ □ □   □□□=93
estamation.
8tt 20=60

The way I got $69 is by using the total, part, part and showing my work and barrowing.

□□ □=24
□□ □□□□

| | total $93 | |
| Part $24 | diffence $69 | |

8 tens ones
$93   13
-$2   4
$6   9

Great opening problems explicitly require students to activate their background knowledge.

Figure 6.1b *Day Starter*

Part B

The Millennium Falcon Lego set that Zaynie wants to buy costs $140. How much more money does Zaynie have to save to in order to buy this Lego set?

Background Knowledge: What do I already know that will help me solve the problem?

I know that Zaynie wants to buy The Millennium Falcon Lego set.

Solve the problem using pictures, numbers and or words

$$\begin{array}{r} \$7\,1 \\ +\$6\,9 \\ \hline \$13\,0 \\ \$\ 1\,0 \\ \hline 1\ 4\,0 \end{array}$$

10's 1's

⎕⎕ ⎕ ⎕⎕⎕⎕ₒ =$71   ⎕⎕⎕⎕⎕⎕
⎕ₒₒ⎕⎕⎕⎕⎕⎕
= $69

I got $140 is by using partial sums and remember that 70+60=130 and 1+9=10

I did 71+69=|

This may mean posing questions that invite thinking—"What do you know about negative exponents?"—rather than solutions—"Find $4^{-3} + 6^{-2}$," though both kinds have their place. Let us explore two approaches that can serve the purpose of activating prior knowledge: Problems of the Day and Conceptual Conversations (though you will see opportunities for them to blend and overlap).

Problem of the Day

As the young teacher described earlier, I thought that the reason students weren't completing the problem of the day was that I wasn't holding them accountable, so I added structures—stamping their notebooks, randomly calling on students to share strategies and answers, and more frequent notebook checks. Though this did increase the participation of some students, I saw no change still in the behavior of about one-third of my class. On probing, I realized that this was because I was asking them to do things they really still did not know how to do. So, whether they were going to miss out on getting a picture of a tarantula rubber stamped on their paper or not was inconsequential; they did not know how to begin.

You have seen those questions that have parts a, b, c, and d and so forth. Sometimes the letters are just that, steps, guiding a dependent learner to complete an otherwise too-tough task: ¾ – ⅓. (a) find the common denominator; then (b) find equivalent fractions, then (c) do the subtraction. This sort of a tiered problem is more like a paint-by-numbers exercise than an opportunity for student thinking, though there is a place for each.

Rather than presenting stepping-stones of that sort, we can offer students problems that invite challenge by choice: Let the first question be something everyone will likely know, followed by questions of increasing complexity that may feed into one another, reminding learners of the concepts behind the mathematics. We can then invite learners to begin where they wish and answer those questions they feel ready to tackle. In this way, we offer everyone a foothold, as well as some decision-making power. For example, if the study is exponents, we may try:

a. What is an exponent?

b. Draw a visual representation of 5^2.

c. Draw a visual representation of 2^3.

d. How would you find $5^2 - 2^3$?

This question may appear similar to the fraction subtraction example above, but the difference is that it asks students, at each step, to *show what they know*, rather than to follow a procedure.

Although your curriculum and materials may provide tiered questions for your use, you may also need to write your own. If you do so, you might start with typical quiz questions, think about the concepts they are based upon, and invite learners to represent those concepts and build toward the solution. Think about what all learners in the room can answer about a mathematical situation, and then progress to more complex analysis and solutions. So, if we go back to ¾ − ⅓, a tiered problem might ask:

a. What is a fraction?

b. Represent ¾ in two or more ways.

c. Represent ⅓ in two or more ways.

d. How would you find ¾ − ⅓?

This last question (d) leaves open the possibility that there are a number of ways of approaching that situation and that students are welcome to think about it in the way that makes sense to them.

Tiered problems of this sort invite the use of thinking strategies, as described in Chapter 2. "What is a fraction?" draws upon students' prior knowledge; "Represent ¾" invites them to create a mental model of this concept that is meaningful to them. These sorts of scaffolds support students in slowing down and understanding problems, a transferable skill. In this way, we offer explicit opportunities for learners to, as the Common Core Standards of Mathematical Practice describe, make sense of problems, as well as model with mathematics in the context of our content explorations.

Once students have created their own mental models, there is great value in taking the time to share those with the group: One at a time, invite a few students up to the front of the room with their work. Step aside as they show and explain what they did. Ask the group to respond, "What did you think of Emily's work? What questions do you have for Emily? How does what Emily did compare to your thinking about this?" and then, inviting the next learner, we can ask, "Did anyone think of this in a different way?" If no one takes that bait, you can try, "So, everyone in here did it exactly the same way as Emily?" The discussion of the opening problem need not be long, but some discourse at this juncture is a wonderful, ritual affirming to learners that math class is about them and their thinking.

Conceptual Conversations Alternately, rather than asking students to solve a problem, we might focus their energies entirely on considering a concept or set of concepts. Let's listen in as Michael Dennis at Shelby West Middle School in Shelbyville, Kentucky, uses his opening routine to activate students' prior knowledge:

> *"Our project today is about what I'm going to be doing over fall break—*
> *retiling my floor. The first thing I'm going to need to do is activate some*

background knowledge." On the SMART Board, he projects a graphic organizer, a grid with eight boxes, then hands out a matching one to each student. The boxes are labeled "area," "mixed number," "multiplying fractions," "area model," "rectangle," "improper fraction," "simplifying fractions," "installing flooring."

"I'm going to give you four minutes—thirty seconds per box—to fill in as much background knowledge as you can. If you have to skip, that's okay. Conversation level zero. I just want to see what you know."

After a few minutes of independent thinking and writing time when learners jot notes on their own papers, Mr. Dennis calls the group back together. "I noticed that a lot of us for area put length x width. Is that always the case?"

"It's for a rectangle," a student offers.

"So we've got to remember to be specific," Mr. Dennis clarifies. "Now we're going to share some of our background knowledge. Find someone with the same color hair and stand back to back. We're going to do two things. When I say go turn around and share the thing you feel you know the most about, you say, 'I feel I know the most about _____ because _____.' Also say the one you know least about: 'The one I know the least about is _____.'"

Students begin to share, "I said rectangle because it has four sides, it's a polygon, it's a parallelogram, all ninety-degree angles, quadrilateral."

"The one I don't know is mixed number."

"I don't know what area model is."

"What did you say about area?"

"I said . . ."

"I put that, except I put it in words."

In this opening, Mr. Dennis did many helpful things: He acknowledged and invited students to share their background knowledge, he made it okay not to know everything, and he created opportunities for learners to connect and talk about vocabulary terms. In a moment, we will see how Mr. Dennis used this task to launch his minilesson and work time.

Planning an Opening Problem or Question
Planning your opening, you might consider inviting students to examine

- a new problem
- a problem from their homework

- recent class work

- a concept central to the unit of study.

In the table below are some questions you could ask, either as part of a specific problem-solving task or in preparation for a conceptual conversation. Note that these questions address important practices as well as thinking skills (making models, critiquing reasoning, and solving problems) and are closely intertwined with, not distinct from, the Common Core State Standard practices.

These are just a few ideas to get you started. Any question that gets students engaged and thinking is a good question.

	About a Problem	**About a Concept**
Background knowledge	What does this problem remind you of?	What do you already know about pyramids?
Asking questions	What are all the questions you can ask about this problem?	What questions do you have about pyramids?
Determining importance	What would be important to think about if you were going to solve this problem? What data are significant? Where would you begin?	What is important to remember about surface area?
Inferring	What might be some stumbling blocks to solving this problem?	How is the concept of surface area used in daily life?
Mental models	Represent this situation in two or more ways.	Create a model to represent what you know about pyramids.
Monitoring for meaning	(Given a solution to a problem.) Does this answer make sense? Why or why not? Explain.	What do you understand now about pyramids? What is confusing about them?
Synthesis	How does this relate to other things we know?	What do triangles have to do with pyramids?

Accountability Structure You can offer the friendliest question in the world, but if learners are not in the routine of participating, those first five minutes of class will be a forum for frustration. How can we efficiently and effectively get students to actually participate? Maybe as you read about Mr. Dennis' class, you are thinking you would not want students to get up, walk around, and talk with each other, for risk of losing their focus completely. Our classroom culture of thinking is supported when we hold all students accountable for participating in all learning activities. We can do so, in part, by carefully structuring the task.

Well-designed structures create an opportunity for a teacher or a classmate, or both, to read what learners wrote or hear what students have been thinking or talking about. In the example above, students wrote individually, then shared with partners. You might invite students to document and share their responses to your queries in a variety of ways. Here are some ideas:

- Thinking Pass: Each student starts with her own piece of paper, responds, then passes that sheet to the next person for them to add their thinking. Can continue several rounds before papers are returned to original author, who then synthesizes all ideas collected.

- Weekly Tracker: Record thinking on a page that has space for each day's opening question, as well as space to revise and add to one's thinking over the course of a study.

- Give One–Get One: Each student, on a paper numbered 1–10, writes four answers to an open-ended question. Then, students mingle, pair, and share: each partner gives one of their first four ideas away, then records one idea they get from each partner on a numbered line below.

- Trios: Invite students to get into groups of three to discuss a topic, then call upon whomever you'd like to share.

- Warm Calling: After individual work time or small-group conversation, call on whomever you like to present to the group. Let learners know that you expect them to be thinking and talking about the topic at hand and to be accountable for sharing their insight.

- Math Notebooks: Learners track their thinking in notebooks, which the teacher collects, reads, and responds to at regular intervals.

Time An opening problem or conversation ought not to consume more than a few minutes, though if not thoughtfully crafted and carefully facilitated, it can easily happen. Ideally, the opening can open students' minds to the topic of the day, generate some thinking and energy, then serve as a springboard into the minilesson. These purposes can be completed in six to eight minutes, if instructions are crisp, transitions are brisk, and accountability is clear.

Of course, new routines need time and modeling to establish, so introducing a new ritual may require some investment of minutes, knowing that later the same routine can be executed more efficiently.

Students Setting Purpose

The opening routine not only helps students activate their prior knowledge; it also serves as a key opportunity to establish purpose for the class period. This purpose may be set by the teacher, or even more effectively, set by the learners themselves.

In Mr. Dennis' class, after the students shared their background knowledge, he proceeded as follows:

> *"I noticed you all don't know a lot about how to install flooring. How are you going to help me solve my problem if you don't know a lot about how to install flooring—but I have an answer.*

> *"This is an article about how to install flooring. I want you to read and annotate. Don't stress if you don't finish. We're just trying to build background knowledge so you can help me solve my problem. Conversation level 0. Go."*

See how his opening channeled students right into his purpose for the next task?

Educational research demonstrates the value of conveying our daily purpose to students. Rick Stiggins (1996) discerned that students make greater progress toward content learning goals when they are aware of a lesson's purpose. Unfortunately, numerous well-intended educators have converted research on the importance of assessment into the practice of requiring overworked teachers to scrawl learning targets on the upper corner of the whiteboard each day, then press on with business as usual. Although there is nothing wrong with jotting targets up there, the point of this act is lost if we do not also take the time to explain to students in kid-friendly terms the actual reason they might like to pursue the day's study and offer students opportunities to own the purpose of the day's work for themselves. Not only do teachers need to be clear about purpose, but more importantly, learners do as well.

As Stiggins described in a 1999 interview with the Journal of Staff Development entitled "Assessment Without Victims,"

> When students are involved in the assessment process, though,
> they can come to see themselves as competent learners. We need
> to involve students by making the targets clear to them and having
> them help design assessments that reflect those targets. Then
> we involve them again in the process of keeping track over time
> of their learning so they can watch themselves improving. That's
> where motivation comes from. (Sparks 1999)

So, as the teacher, I certainly need to state the learning target. But even more importantly, I need to then invite learners to set intentions for *themselves*. This can be done in age-appropriate ways at any grade level:

> *Ninth-grade teacher Tracey Shaw at Smokey Hill High School devotes time
> to ensuring that students understand learning targets, assess their own
> progress toward those, and then, based upon their self-assessment, determine their purpose regularly. In opening a class devoted to review for an
> upcoming quiz, she invites learners to refer to the unit's learning targets
> and consider their own individual areas of strength and weakness.*

> *"I want you to star the two things you need to work on," she instructs
> students as they review the targets. Then, as she distributes a packet of
> review questions, she explains, "This is not due until Monday, but we're
> used to just starting with the first problem, and losing steam. Don't be
> afraid to start with the sections you're struggling with most. Do those today or tomorrow so you can come to the review session. Leave the easier
> stuff to the weekend. Have a game-plan for preparing."*

By inviting students to honestly assess their own abilities and needs, Ms. Shaw ensures that all move purposefully into the work time.

When working with adult learners, I often tell the story of my own grocery shopping, how I may go into the store looking for bread and jam, but find myself wandering down an aisle full of pickles. Though I don't like pickles, I don't fret about how much grocery aisle real estate is devoted to featuring vinegared cucumbers and instead devote my attention to finding what I need and want: bread and jam. My purpose was not just to go to the store, but rather to get bread and jam. Anything distracting me from that purpose is a waste of time.

Similarly, a student's purpose as a math learner in any given class ought to be more than getting through the lesson, but rather exercising a growth mindset, mastering content, and also honing her endurance as a problem solver, as well as her skills as a thinker. When we invite learners to look at an agenda for the day then to set a goal for themselves, they can consciously proceed through a lesson with purpose of their own.

This does not mean to throw the doors open wide for learners to pick any old target. Rather, teachers must first establish a destination—finding arithmetic means, for example. Then, within that framework, aware of the activity of the day— say, examining a family's annual spending by category month to month—think about how they might structure that task to ensure all students access to this purpose.

Once this planning work is done, teachers are ready to invite students to establish their *own* purpose: What do you need to get smarter about? What do you need to work on? Precision? Patience?

For students to establish their own purpose in a day's lesson or a week's work, we can orient learners to the plan and then ask questions like:

- What do you know for sure?

- What are you confused about?

- What do you need to get better at?

- What do you most need to pay attention to as a problem solver?

- What kinds of questions do you predict you should be prepared to answer?

And why ought they care? It may not actually be that we can connect anything in a study of mean-median-mode to skateboarding, though we might feel obliged to do so. Although some mathematics is clearly connected with and relevant to students' daily lives, other aspects are less so. In these cases, we might answer the relevance question by reminding students of the Common Core Math Practices: An ability to reason abstractly and quantitatively, for example, will hopefully outlive a student's capacity to accurately construct a box and whisker plot freehand.

Purpose can be established quickly (Dennis) or more slowly (Shaw) but needs to be attended to and revisited regularly to motivate all math learners to engage meaningfully each day.

Managing Homework

In addition to welcoming students, making connections to prior knowledge, and setting purpose, most teachers want to do something with students' homework toward the beginning of class, whether collect it, correct it, or discuss it. Starting class by looking at homework can be a great approach that does indeed activate prior knowledge: This habit can reinforce the expectation that homework is a ticket into class, clarify lingering doubts about the content, and orient students to where they have been and where they are headed in their math learning. Alternately, some teachers elect not to start class by reviewing homework, lest students should feel immediately evaluated and perhaps discouraged. If you do choose to put time into homework at the outset, here are a few strategies for checking homework efficiently:

- Tally check: High school teacher Tracey Shaw has a simple system for checking homework without going over problem after problem: She writes a list of the problem numbers on the board, and in the first few minutes of class invites students to put a tally mark next to any they'd like help with. Then, she chooses the two to three problems with which most students struggled, and uses those as fodder for a few minutes of group discussion.

- Share and compare: Rather than giving answers, some teachers elect to put students into small groups to look over their work then discuss one or more discrepant answers. This requires students to justify their thinking and defend their solutions in a quest to understand how to complete all problems correctly.

- Clickers: Invite students to enter homework answers using clickers, then look together at the data collected and decide which problems to discuss as a group.

- Weekly quiz: Check, but don't collect or grade the homework. Instead, give a quiz each week that includes one or more problems from each day's homework. If learners did and understood the homework, they will ace the quiz.

In terms of grading homework, think about what is important to you, and give your points based on that. Do you value accuracy? Effort? Completeness? Maybe you don't have time to read everyone's whole paper in full so you just want to give points for question 10. Alternately, some teachers decide that homework is mere practice, and that students get points for homework by doing well on tests and other assessments.

Alternately, master middle school math teacher Deb Maruyama gives little to no homework. "Things I do send home are arithmetic, total independent practice. Don't dwell on homework very much," she advises.

"Yeah, but . . ."

"Why not just jump right in to the minilesson, rather than using up all this time?"

Some teachers choose not to start with a problem for students to work on or to do so only from time to time. The opening routine, as described above, is not a prescription, but a suggestion: When we start class by inviting and encouraging student thinking, we convey to learners the important message that this class is about their working to hone ideas and solve problems.

"Do I need to do a problem and talk about purpose every day?"

It is helpful to devote time to both, but not necessarily exhaustively, and not necessarily in equal measure each day. Go back to the question of what you want your students to experience and feel as the class begins, and create an opening that is aligned with those goals.

"How do I manage the paperwork of the daily problems?"

Some teachers have students turn in their problems daily, but most have some sort of daily check (stamp, etc.) and then collect students' work either weekly or less often. If you invite students to work in math notebooks, you might just collect five of those each day, review the previous week's work, then collect another five from the group the next day. It is a lot to stay on top of, but it is important that if we ask students to write their thinking, we also create an audience for that writing.

Quod Erat Demonstrandum

Learners' first few minutes in our classrooms should be about *them* thinking, talking, writing, focusing. These minutes send important messages about what we value, expect, and hope. When we start class by welcoming learners, we let them know we are glad to have them there. As we activate their prior knowledge, we remind them of what they already know about concepts, and then by inviting them to channel their energy toward a learning purpose all their own, we honor their individuality and demonstrate respect for their different needs. All of this can be accomplished in a thoughtful opening that will segue smoothly into your minilesson.

CHAPTER 7

Minilessons

If we see ourselves predominantly as teachers of curriculum—
even exemplary curriculum—we have forgotten half of our professional role.
We are teachers of human beings. The essence of our job is making sure
that the curriculum serves as a catalyst for powerful learning
for our students who, with our guidance and support,
become skilled in and committed to the process of learning.

—*Carol Ann Tomlinson and Jay McTighe,*
Integrating Differentiated Instruction and Understanding by Design

Problem of the Day: How do you set students up for success as independent thinkers and problem solvers?

Postulate: We apprentice learners as mathematicians by explicitly teaching students how mathematicians use thinking strategies, make sense of and apply concepts to help them solve problems.

Some of us started teaching math because we like it and we are good at it. This was my downfall as a first-year teacher: I had no idea what could possibly be confusing about probability because it just made tremendous sense to me. Plus, I was mystified as to why every preteen in my room was not riveted by the opportunity to calculate the chances of pulling out a purple sock then a red one from a specific collection. There was such lovely logic to it all. I could illustrate with pictures or numbers or models exactly why I was right every time. But a crazy thing was happening: The more I explained, the less my students seemed to understand. The more sample problems I did for them, the sleepier they appeared.

Then, when I sent them off to do their practice worksheets, a forest of arms would reach for the ceiling; sometimes half the class at once would put their hands in the air seeking assistance. I'd gladly sit down with each table group to help. Here's how it went: I'd explain number one, and then they would all write my answer down. Then I would demonstrate number two, and they would all write that answer as well. But when I slipped away to help another group, then returned, I'd too often find the first table of beleaguered students exactly where I had left them, on number two.

I was feeling really good at math. But meanwhile, my students were only getting smart about how to run the game of my class. They figured out that if they played dumb long enough, I would tell them all the answers. I was doing all the heavy lifting, and no one was learning much math at all.

In the short run, it is easier, faster, and tidier to do the work for students. But what if someone's flotation device pops in the deep end? What about when students are alone sitting for the SAT? Ultimately, we *do* want students to learn to succeed independently, right? So we need to stop doing the work for them.

If student independence is the goal, then, these guys are going to need proper swimming lessons, the kind where we show them what to do, then let go of them in the water to experience what it really takes to float. Without water wings.

Any swimming teacher knows, though, that you can't just give a demo on the pool deck, then chuck the kids in the water. Independence comes in small steps. So it can be with math, as well, starting with a minilesson.

Teach the Mathematician

A minilesson is quick and strategically designed to support students in developing acuity as independent mathematicians: a short, focused segment of whole-group instruction led by the teacher for ten or fewer minutes. The end goal of a minilesson is to prepare learners for independence. We do so by providing essential information and modeling the tools for thinking and problem solving that students will need to succeed. The minilesson can then be seen as the theatre for both demonstration and inspiration.

In typical instruction, a teacher simply tells students how to work a problem: "So, you take the equation for circumference and plug in six for the radius, then multiply. . . ." Minilessons involve unpacking ideas to reveal the mysterious mental moves behind the mathematician's solution: "So, I am asking myself, what do I know, and what do I need to find out? I know that the distance around a circle is called its circumference. . . . "

Modeling Thinking Versus Showing Examples

Modeling thinking—sometimes referred to as *thinking aloud*—is the key to a successful minds-on math workshop and an integral aspect of a minilesson. This is the time when a teacher cracks open the black box of her brain and unveils that magic of her thought processes. Students witnessing such a model come to understand not only *how* to solve a problem but also *why* that strategy works and how a mathematician might reason her way to such a solution.

Typical Instruction: Showing Examples Often, teachers show several examples to students before releasing them to independent work. A typical example may go something like this:

> "So, we have x − 3 = 11," the teacher says as she jots the equation on the board. "What do I need to do?"
>
> "Get x by itself," a student calls out.
>
> "Right," the teacher affirms. "How do I get x by itself?"
>
> "Subtract three from both sides." Another student volunteers.
>
> "Subtract?" the teacher asks.
>
> "Add!" a third student offers up.
>
> "Yes!" the teacher agrees. "We add three to both sides." The teacher goes ahead and writes "+3" on each side of the equation, then invites the students' help. "So, what's 11 + 3?"
>
> A chorus responds. "Fourteen."
>
> "Right," the teacher confirms. "x = 14."

Sound familiar?

Minilesson: Modeling Thinking Let's listen in and hear how a teacher might use the same problem to more explicitly model thinking:

> "x − 3 = 11," the teacher writes on the board. "So, I am thinking that in order to make sense of this statement, which is what mathematicians do, make sense of problems and persevere in solving them, I am going to need to start with my background knowledge. I know that it is an equa-

*tion because it has an equals sign and tells me that something (x − 3)
equals something else (11). I also know that I am being asked to do some
algebra and solve this equation, which means find out what x is worth.
So, I am using my background knowledge to help me think about what
kind of math this is and what I am supposed to do with this question. Do
you have any other background knowledge that you think might help me
solve this problem?"*

The teacher records her background knowledge in another color next to the equation.

"You have to get x by itself," a student offers.

"Why?" the teacher probes.

*"I remember from when we talked about equations last year that it's like
a puzzle, and you have to undo everything until you get x by itself. That's
how you find out what x is worth."*

*"Aha, so Kian has some background knowledge about how to solve this
problem. He is remembering from last year that we need to take steps to
isolate x, which means get x all by itself."*

As she affirms his thinking, the teacher also adds to their list of background knowledge.

In this way, the teacher launched the minilesson by sharing with students how she approaches solving problems of this nature. After a demonstration and discussion, the group summarized her minilesson, noticing aloud what they observed her doing:

- Started with background knowledge.
- Made a plan to get *x* by itself.
- Did the same thing to both sides.
- Did the opposite to get rid of the minus three.

When she asked about potential pitfalls they might encounter as problem solvers, they offered:

- *Get scared when you see the x.*

- *Undo the wrong thing.*

- *Forget how to do the opposite.*

- *Make a silly booboo (arithmetic mistakes).*

In this way, the teacher invited learners to understand her problem-solving processes from the inside out, to articulate the replicable aspects of her work, and to note any challenges they might find when pursuing similar problems.

When we examine the differences between these two minilessons about $x - 3 = 11$, we can grasp the key difference: typical instruction is all about giving a child a fish, while minilessons are about teaching children how to fish.

What's the Lesson?

Rather than devoting time to rehearsing an algorithm, such as the mechanics of lattice multiplication, a minilesson gives priority to modeling strategies and habits of mind that can enhance learners' work as self-sufficient mathematicians. A minilesson may target math content, math process skills, strategies for successful collaboration, or any other specific understanding that learners need to be prepared for the independent or small-group work of work time. You could use your minilesson to:

- offer direct instruction of content, such as new vocabulary

- revisit the findings of the previous day's workshop, for example, clarify what students understand about similar triangles

	Typical Instruction	**Minilesson**
Big Idea	"Here's how to **do** this math."	"Here's how to **think** as a mathematician about this situation."
Content	◆ demonstrates procedures, doing ◆ shows answer ◆ invites students to complete calculations	◆ models reasoning process, thinking ◆ explicitly demonstrates thinking strategy(ies) ◆ focuses on reasoning and understanding ◆ invites students to share thinking ◆ summarizes key learnings

- introduce a thinking strategy, perhaps background knowledge

- model the use of a problem-solving strategy, such as inferring

- discuss the implementation of a specific mathematical practice, such as precision

- revisit community agreements

- discuss the relevance of a particular concept to learners' lives.

In selecting the focus of a minilesson, a teacher reviews the learning goals of the unit, considers the formative assessment data gathered during the previous class session, and decides what learners need most to move forward. Minilessons build on one another throughout the course of a unit of study, as well as over a semester.

Minilessons on Problem Solving

Most commonly, minds-on math workshops begin with a minilesson targeting students' thinking and problem-solving skills. To this end, a fine-tuned minilesson includes a content focus paired with an appropriate process focus. For example, I recently planned an algebra lesson for a group of students exploring exponents. In the minilesson, I introduced them to the idea of mental models and discussed how mathematicians use mental models to understand situations. I gave an example of how I had used a mental model (a map) in my own life to solve a problem, and then we brainstormed a list of possible mental models one could use; then, during work time, I offered students the Rabbits and Pythons problem (see Appendix B) and asked them to create their own mental models to illustrate the situation. Students were prepared for independent work: They understood what mental models were in general, they had seen one example of a mental model specifically applied, and on the board was a brainstormed list of potential mental models they could choose to use in their work. Everyone got started.

When we are using a minilesson to launch independent problem solving of this sort, it is helpful to plan for some or all of the following:

> ## Why "Mini"?
>
> Gone are the days when a rapt group of teens sits attentively while a teacher explains, describes, models, and elaborates on a point of mathematical interest for forty-five minutes on end. Plus, if we use up the entire class period lecturing, there is no time left for students to get to work—which is how we want to spend the majority of our time in a minds-on math workshop. In fact, brain scientist Dr. John Medina's research synthesis (2008) indicates that after ten minutes, we see a significant decrease in listeners' attention unless we intentionally take action to reengage our audience.
>
> According, again, to Medina, the most common communication error we humans—not just teachers—make is "relating too much information with not enough time devoted to connecting the dots. Lots of force feeding, very little digestion" (2008, 103). So, in addition to being "mini" in the amount of time it takes, a minilesson ought also to be devoted to a singular learning target—or perhaps two—then followed by opportunities for students to test approaches, synthesize ideas, and construct understanding. Carefully designed, targeted minilessons leave ample time for students to do the work of thinking during class.

- explicit instruction on thinking strategy or mathematical practice
- a parallel problem
- opportunities for student engagement and thinking
- pursuit of misconceptions
- debrief and reflection.

Explicit Thinking Strategy or Mathematical Practice

In addition to being an opportunity to explain and demonstrate content, a minilesson is also the key juncture to introduce or refresh a specific strategy or practice, as described in Chapter 2. In introducing a new skill or strategy, we can offer students an array of means to experience, understand, and remember what it is and how it might be useful for their math learning. We might spread exposure to one specific strategy over the course of a unit of study, peppering our minilessons with various strategy-related experiences, one at a time, including:

- offering real-life examples (ours and theirs)
- sketching anchor charts
- explaining in the context of math
- thinking aloud—making our thinking transparent
- showing ways to hold thinking (tailored to the strategy).

Let's give it a try.

Real-Life Examples When introducing a new strategy or practice, it is helpful for learners to realize that this is not a brand-new way of thinking they have never tried before, but a familiar habit you are now inviting them to put to work in service of math learning.

For example, if you were introducing the strategy of background knowledge, you might tell the story of how your background knowledge helped you to find your way when you were lost downtown amid one-way streets in a snowstorm: You knew that Logan St. headed north, so if you crossed Logan, and it was going to your right, you were heading west. After telling examples of your own, you can invite learners to recall their own experiences using background knowledge to make sense of situations; let them see that this is something they already know how to do.

Anchor Charts An anchor chart is like a one-frame cartoon that reminds us what a strategy means. These can be fun to sketch and discuss and hang in the classroom as visual reminders of one of the tools in our thinking toolbox.

For background knowledge, you might sketch thinking bubbles inside a brain lighting up when the thinker is prompted by the outside world. For questioning, you might depict a mind brainstorming all of the question words. For synthesizing, you might draw ideas cooking over time. Talk with your students about what images and metaphors would help them remember each strategy, and use those illustrations to decorate your classroom.

Explaining in the Context of Math Once we have talked about the strategies in general and represented them visually, we need to quickly think through how these can be useful to us as math learners. We can certainly use our own examples to tell learners what role a strategy has played in our lives as mathematicians: I filled out my tax return, and it said I owed thousands of dollars to the IRS. Based on my background knowledge—I had taken only two exemptions and almost always got a refund—I knew that I must have made a mistake. We can also invite them to think for themselves about how this strategy might be useful to us in math learning.

Thinking Aloud After these games with a strategy—talking about it, drawing it, trying it on for size—it is time to show students exactly how to put it to work. This is best done during our minilesson as a *think-aloud*. The think-aloud is that opportunity we have to take our unconscious processes as a mathematician and to make them conscious, clear, and apparent to our audience of learners. Thinking aloud means telling the story of what happens in our minds as we apply a strategy to a situation. Let's try determining importance:

> *I project the problem onto the Promethean and have a go on chart paper:*
>
> *"It says, 'Find the missing side lengths.'" I read as I gaze at the L-shaped figure with only a few sides labeled. "And at first I am thinking, how can I possibly do that? I hardly have any information. But then, I remember that I have to keep up my stamina, that there must be a way . . . so, now I am wondering, what is really important here that can help me solve the problem?*
>
> *"I know that I can take a compound figure like this and divide it into smaller parts to find the area. I am wondering if that might also help me to find the missing side." I go ahead and draw lines and divide the figure into one square in the corner and two rectangles.*
>
> *"Hmm," I lean back. "Did that help me? I know both sides of a square are equal and that these measurements have to equal those." I point to the adjacent sides. "I think that is important."*

And so forth. By modeling in this way, we can show students that problem solving involves a variety of thinking and effort and is not always a straight path but can be streamlined by the application of a specific and intentional strategy.

Showing Ways to Hold Thinking In addition to thinking aloud to model the thought process, we can also use that think-aloud to model a means of documenting thinking. Whether margin notes, sketches, graphic organizers, or otherwise, students benefit from observing and integrating transferable means to document what they understand and how they proceed through a problem.

Parallel Problems

A strong minilesson may include one or more carefully selected sample problems. This act of apprenticing learners to your own thinking processes as a teacher allows students to observe, discuss, and potentially emulate your thinking in another context. Rather than showing a sample problem that precisely matches the work students are about to do (that is, find the probability of finding a nonpurple sock from a collection, then ask learners to find the probability of finding a purple sock from the same group), we can instead use what I call a "parallel problem." A parallel problem is one that offers exposure to similar or related thinking without "giving away" the task of their work time. So, if learners are about to embark on solving a problem about the tortoise and the hare, rather than starting that same problem for them during the minilesson, you might introduce a simpler problem about a jogger and a bicycle rider, and let them talk it through together before heading off to work. When we choose a simpler, parallel problem to model, students can track and understand our thinking, then strive to translate it to the unique challenges to come.

Opportunities for Student Engagement and Thinking

In the typical algebra example at the beginning of this chapter, the teacher invited students' suggestions as to how to solve the problem (without asking why) and devoted time only to correct answers. In a minilesson, though we are modeling, we can pause and we seek students' participation in ways that support their mathematical thinking and conceptual understanding. At intervals, we can ask students to:

- turn and talk to a partner, "What is a variable?"
- show with their thumbs whether they understand the content so far: "Thumbs up if you understand why I just subtracted three from both sides; thumbs down if you don't"

- comment on our work or thinking

- elaborate on their comments by responding to probing questions: "Why?" or "Say more."

In these ways, students are more than simply an audience to our brilliance but become engaged as thinkers throughout the minilesson.

Pursuit of Misconceptions

As teachers, when a student shares an error, we often want to rush to the correct solution. Yet in her valuable piece, "What's Right About Looking at What's Wrong" (2007), Deborah Schifter points out the high value of exploring students' misconceptions, illuminating those dark alleys so that all can observe their emptiness. In the example used earlier, the teacher takes the time to invite the group to think about Max's idea—subtracting three from both sides—rather than dismissing it. Stopping to shine the light of day on potential areas of confusion can be helpful to many learners and is well worth the time.

Debrief

At the end, our minilesson teacher asked students to think about how to solve problems of this sort, as well as any pitfalls they thought they might encounter with those. As demonstrated in the $x - 3 = 11$ minilesson, at the end of the minilesson, the teacher gathered and recorded the thinking of the group. This takes time, time that few teachers are anxious to give up, but time well spent increasing students' awareness of how they themselves can take ownership of the problem solving process. Our debrief can be just a simple question or two. These might include:

- What do you need to remember about problems like these?

- What kinds of thinking did we need to do to solve this problem?

- When will you need to be careful on a problem like this?

The previous algebra examples are composite vignettes designed to give you a flavor of both ends of the spectrum—one of merely showing examples and the other of explicitly modeling thinking. Naturally, most of us as teachers fall someplace in between. If our goal, though, is to train students as independent problem solvers, they will benefit most when we plan and facilitate minilessons that contain ample opportunities for students to hear each others' voices.

Checking for Understanding

By both modeling your own thinking and inviting students' engagement and participation, a minilesson guides learners through the first steps of the gradual release of responsibility (Pearson and Gallagher 1983). Once the minilesson is complete, you will want to check for students' understanding and confidence levels before moving into the work time. One time-tested tip: *Please don't* ask, "Does everyone understand?" because in my experience, students compliantly nod and smile in response to this question. Instead, try, "What questions do you have?" This invitation affirms your expectation that your thoughtful growth-minded mathematicians have been working hard to understand throughout the minilesson and that at this juncture they would certainly be expected to have numerous insightful questions. Once you hear their questions, make a prompt plan to address them. This does not mean *you* have to answer them; turn that job over to the group: "How might you all help Ava with her question?"

If you feel pressed for time, you can try any number of quick assessments to decide how students feel about being released to small-group or independent work:

- Fist of Five: Invite students to rate their comprehension on a scale of zero (*don't get it*) to five (*got it!*), and to show you as many fingers.
- Stand-ups: Using this binary system, invite students to stand up if they "get it" and are ready to move on.
- Lineups: Invite students to line up along a wall, with one corner representing total confusion and the opposite representing total mastery.

Based on students' questions or their responses to your quick checkups, you can make decisions about how to proceed. Some students may need additional support after the minilesson to get started on their work for the day. You may choose to put students into groups to wrestle together with challenges, invite some learners to stay together with you for more modeling, or encourage learners to have a go anyhow, and plan to confer promptly with those who seem to lack confidence. At other times, your check for understanding may indicate that you need to loop back and revisit an aspect of the minilesson with the whole group.

Planning over Time

One minilesson is a mere patch in a quilt of experiences that, together, develop students' conceptual understanding. Rather than feeling as though we need to deliver all content at the beginning of the unit before offering students any individual experience with the concepts, we can plan a series of minilessons with both content and process-learning goals that, together, scaffold and support students' mastery.

For example, a study of data displays could be overlaid with the thinking strategy determining importance as follows:

	Minilesson	Work Time	Sharing and Reflection
Monday	Introduce the idea of determining importance by inviting discussion about how and when we determine importance in our own lives.	In small groups, examine graphs and determine what is important about each.	Discuss how we determined importance in the graphs.
Tuesday	Review what we thought was important about graphs yesterday. Briefly describe stations activity.	Stations activity: learn about and create a new data display at each ◆ line graph ◆ scatter plot ◆ box and whisker plot, ◆ histogram ◆ pie graph.	Students reflect by writing about what is important about the data display they learned to create that day.
Wednesday	Look at some student work from previous day's lesson, and discuss whether those graphs include important elements. Consider what else might be important.	Students rotate stations (day two).	Students reflect on work time, as well as why graphs are important and useful.
Thursday	Troubleshoot common errors observable in stations (refer to conferring notes).	Students rotate stations (day three).	Students share work from their favorite station so far.
Friday	Examine *USA Today* graphs and look for bias. Ask how bias relates to determining importance.	Students rotate stations (day four).	Students further articulate what is important about graphs by beginning to create a rubric for a graph.

"Yeah, but . . ."

"Do I have to start class with the minilesson? Sometimes I don't know what students need until they get started."

Many mentor math teachers swap around the order of the segments in their workshops depending on the needs of their students each day. You may try starting class with work time, letting students have a go with a problem to create their need to know the content of an upcoming minilesson. As long as students are engaged in making meaning as mathematicians, there is no "wrong" way to use your minutes.

"Minilessons like these take way too much time."

A minilesson is indeed more time-consuming than showing a quick example or two. Yet, this investment of time is intended to explicitly make students aware of how to think and reason as mathematicians, a worthy investment, and one that pays off in the long run by increasing students' independence.

Our textbook is set up just like this: Launch, Practice, Reflection. What's the difference between this and the workshop model?

This textbook structure can be helpful, yet we need to be mindful that we do not simply repeat the explain–assign model traditionally employed with limited effectiveness. *Launch* can be thought of as an opportunity to model thinking, *Practice* is the work time, and *Reflection* is just that—a chance for learners to reflect on what they came to understand through their practice. As long as each segment is focused on promoting student thinking, this format matches workshop well.

"It doesn't sound like doing this kind of minilesson during a math workshop gives much time for teaching."

Workshop model instruction conceives of teaching differently: Direct instruction time is decreased so that students' opportunities to solve problems and experiment with ideas are increased. Still, windows for differentiated instruction abound. Through conferring during work time, teachers tailor their direct instruction, as described in Chapter 9.

"What about flip teaching? Can I just do the minilesson on video and have students watch it for homework?"

Many teachers are finding online resources can be useful tools for their instruction. Inviting students to watch these can be an efficient strategy for building background knowledge, though video has its limitations. Students will benefit from us taking time in class to explicitly model thinking authentic to the strategies we are teaching in an interactive forum.

Quod Erat Demonstrandum

To apprentice students as thinkers in a minds-on math workshop, we need to explicitly model how our own minds think mathematically and to demonstrate transferable problem-solving strategies. By scaffolding students' understanding of and ability to independently use transferable strategies, we apprentice them in the work of master mathematicians. We can design lessons and units with symbiotic process and content learning goals and invite students to reflect upon their agility with each.

CHAPTER 8

Work Time

Pages of mindless computation do not foster the construction of new knowledge. Learners need the opportunity to collect, generate, and frame their own problems and inquiries. The learner must be in the driver's seat.

—Katherine Merseth, "How Old Is the Shepherd?"

Question of the Day: How can we facilitate thoughtful and productive work time for math learners?

Postulate: Students learn most when they spend math work time thinking, talking, and making meaning of mathematics for themselves.

"So, that's one way we could do it, make a table, but what if we sketched it out . . . like this, and found the volumes?" Joanna asks, then draws a diagram quickly on graph paper to illustrate her thinking about how to find the relationship between a triangular pyramid's base area, its height, and its volume.

"I think we should start with the table—that way, we get all the numbers before we draw it out."

"I need to see it," Joanna asserts. "How about I draw it out, and you make the table."

"Okay, let's both do the same dimensions and make sure we get it right—precision. What should we start with?"

"Base side lengths of one unit."

The two girls hunch over their work, writing, sketching, punching at their calculators. Hushed learners engage in similarly math-focused conversation throughout the room. Their teacher is crouched near one table, coaching those students through their troubles finding square roots.

Every once in a while, I walk into a classroom like this where there is a purposeful, quiet hum; where students are leaning forward into the work on their tables; where conversations consistently focus on math concepts; where everyone knows what to do and is doing it; where the teacher is nearly invisible, and the classroom appears to run itself. This is the dream of work time: self-direction, independence, and purpose as learners delve into rigorous content.

Work time is the lifeblood of the workshop: This is where the learning happens, when students are released to test the mettle of their minds against a steep challenge, to apply their thinking strategies and use the mathematical practices we have been modeling. Yet, student independence can be hard to scaffold—so many learners have grown accustomed to us holding their hand or rescuing them from struggle. For work time to work, we have to let the learners *do* the work with their own good minds. You have laid the groundwork, providing a foundation for their success: a community of learners, a clear minilesson, and an accessible yet challenging task. In addition to providing these advanced supports, teachers as facilitators striving to grow students' stamina as independent mathematicians need to offer clear structure and differentiated support during work time to scaffold students' capacity to manage struggle and maintain motivation.

In this chapter, we will explore four aspects of successful work time:

- planning around rigorous tasks that drive understanding

- planning students' working groups to ensure that all are thinking

- training students to engage as independent mathematicians during work time

- stepping back from helping and instead serving as facilitator and data collector.

Planning for Work Time

In planning for work time, we need to think about two critical aspects: what learners will be doing, and how they will be doing it. In other words, there is the task itself and then the way we organize learners to complete the task. The task and the group arrangement need to be conceived of together. For students to collaborate effectively, their challenge must require all their assets and thinking.

A common misconception is that worksheets can't promote collaboration, but kinesthetic tasks do. As a new teacher, I made the mistake of inventing a sort of round-robin math activity where I took the review worksheet out of our book and cut up the problems and spread them out around the room, each one on its own poster. During class, I put kids in groups and let them scamper around from poster to poster with magic markers, scrawling answers and rushing to the finish line, "reviewing" for the test the next day. I leaned back and smiled, thinking it was terrific—they were all engaged, or so it looked. They bombed the test.

The math problems themselves might have been okay review questions, but it was the structure *around* the task that fell short of scaffolding students' collaboration and thinking: First of all, it was a sort of race, so getting an answer was prioritized over thinking, and groups deferred to their strongest members. Second, there was no accountability. Answers were left behind on posters, not revisited. Third, there was no invitation for metacognition. Students were not spending their time trying to get smarter about anything in particular. If you had Billy in your group, you were psyched: you got to run behind him from table to table, watch him write down answers and feel smart, even though you were not learning. Bad design.

For the next unit, when it came time for a review activity, I had a new plan: expert problem-solving stations. Again, I used the review worksheet from the book; I photocopied it, cut it up, and glued each problem to a piece of colored paper, placing one problem at each table. But my design then diverged: The first group of students would sit down at a station, work on a review problem until they all truly understood the content. Then, that group would get up and move to the next problem station, but, before they left, I would randomly call on one person from each group to stay behind to coach the incoming group. I circulated, checking answers, conferring with groups, making notes about whom I might chat with further individually before the test. With this redesign, I addressed many of the pitfalls of the pandemonium I had created reviewing the previous unit. This use of reciprocal teaching translated into excellent test results, and I continued to employ this structure in the future.

Let us look now at how we can conceive of tasks matched with appropriate structures to engage all learners and hold them accountable for thinking and understanding.

Planning How the Task Will Go

In Chapter 3, we discussed in detail the design of high cognitive demand tasks that challenge students within their zone of proximal development (Vygotsky 1978). Here, let's consider how you might hone a task within the context of a day's workshop for the benefit of a diverse group of learners. For a given workshop to work, the task needs to be sufficiently challenging to each learner so that all students have something interesting and engaging to chew on and talk about.

Now, you are looking at your roster and thinking I am crazy, because we all know that what is high cognitive demand for Maya might blow Megan's circuits and that what is challenging to Jamal could bore Jayden to tears. There is no one-size-fits-all demonstration of understanding of perfectly tuned cognitive demand. But you already knew that. This is why math teachers differentiate. Let us consider how a workshop around a common task might be scaffolded for and experienced differently by diverse learners.

Strategies for Differentiation

The thought of differentiation can be overwhelming; if you are right now envisioning your thirty-two students each having their own ILP, stop and think instead about groups of learners with similar needs and consider how differentiation can help you tweak a common, shared task to facilitate maximum student learning. That is, everyone in the room might be working at the same time on decimals, and even completing similar tasks, though the ways and means may differ for some learners.

Carol Ann Tomlinson (Tomlinson and Tighe 2006) offers us three distinct strategies for differentiation informed by three specific reasons to differentiate: We can differentiate content, product, or process based on student affect, readiness, and interest.

Before we apply these to math, let's try them out on a hike up Colorado's 14,265-foot Mt. Evans: differentiation by *content* would allow advanced students to run ahead. Perhaps some students would be waylaid practicing their walking before being released to hit the trail. My favorite aspect of differentiating by content is differentiation by *complexity*: differentiation by complexity invites us to consider how far from the finish line we draw the starting line and what tools or challenges might evoke the most appropriate experience for each individual or group.

Differentiation by *product* could allow all mountaineers to document their trek to the summit in their own way and to be assessed on that documentation. They might earn points for their photographic essays, water color paintings, or three-dimensional models of their route.

Differentiation by *process* would invite various students to reach the summit in ways best suited to their strengths and needs: Some might hike the trail, others bike the road, a few head up a cliff and scale an off-width crack while on belay. If departures were well orchestrated, everyone could arrive at the top near the same time with their own unique tales of high adventure to tell.

	Content	Product	Process
Strategies for differentiation	◆ Changing the numbers in a problem ◆ Adjusting the reading level of the text ◆ Adding layers or steps to finding a solution ◆ Giving different amounts of work to different groups	◆ Flexibility with how learners demonstrate understanding ◆ Choice in final format ◆ Clear descriptors of quality ◆ Intentional scaffolding	◆ Breaking tasks into small steps ◆ Choice in whether to partner, and with whom ◆ Choice of resource materials ◆ Choice of problem-solving strategies ◆ Choice of mental models

Now that I have dragged you with me on my last hike of the summer, let us consider what each of these approaches might mean in math.

Differentiation by Content

When I was a kid, most math teachers differentiated by content. That is, the "advanced" students could skip easy problems (just do the odds), do extra extensions at the end of the chapter, or even work ahead in the book at their own pace. Typically, in these instances, the "average" students continued their daily work from the textbook, and the keener students got to try some interesting applied math and construct balsa wood models unsupervised.

Sometimes this sort of differentiation by content works really well—the motivated students just plain go faster and get to cover more material. But sometimes, not so well: A decade ago, I inherited a group of gifted seventh graders who had already "learned" algebra in sixth grade. Essentially, their teacher had sent a handful of them into the hallway with some algebra books while she taught math to the remainder of the class. This seemed to work well for both the teacher and the algebra group— but not so well for me, the teacher who had to inform them that chatting with your friends for thirty minutes a day with a heavy book in your lap did not actually equate to learning.

So, here's the problem of differentiating by content: It fractures the learning community, stifles discourse, and makes the teachers' job so complex that she may be tempted to write off a few quiet-in-the-hall kids to tend to the really critical cases. How can we minimize this sort of mathematical triage?

We can hold the content constant and adjust for complexity by creating three versions of the same problem: If your purpose is for students to practice finding areas of compound shapes, all three versions of your task sheet might look the same, though the most accessible will have figures labeled with one-digit numbers, then the medium level of challenge will offer learners a task sheet whose dimensions are in two-digit numbers, and the most sophisticated learners' sheet will invite them to calculate areas using dimensions that include decimals. In this way, all learners are striving toward mastering the same conceptual skill—finding areas—yet are practicing computational skills within their zone of proximal development.

Differentiation by Product *Differentiation by product* means offering students different ways to show what they understand about a concept (similarity of geometric figures) or their solution to a problem (using similar figures to calculate the height of tall objects based on their shadow lengths and the known heights of other objects).

We can think about changing the products we ask learners to complete from unit to unit or about giving students a choice in how they present their thinking. As described by Quate and McDermott in *Clockwatchers* (2010), choice is one of six key steps to motivating and engaging disengaged learners, so, when it is reasonable, we can invite learners to have some say in how they will show what they know. Ultimately, students do not all need to do the exact same thing to show that they understand.

Differentiation by Process We cannot offer students bicycles, skateboards, scooters, and running shoes to differentiate the route to mathematical understanding, so what might differentiation by process look like? *Differentiation by process* means adjusting how learners accomplish the learning task and understanding goal: Some may be doing work in their head while others write it out; some may need more time and practice on specific skills than others; some may need additional representations and visual models to understand. You probably already have a deep bank of strategies for differentiation by process. These can include offering students resources and supports suited to their abilities. Resources could include manipulatives, tools, or calculators, and support might include collaborating with peers in their first language, additional skills practice using computer software, or conferring with adults.

For example, say you are striving to support all students in understanding operations with positive and negative numbers, and the task of the day is to solve and illustrate a series of word problems involving positive and negative numbers. Rather than insisting that all students use the same mental model to work through these sorts of problems, we can instead make a variety of materials available and welcome students to solve problems in the ways that make sense to them: with chips, on a number line, drawing and erasing, and so forth. All children get to construct

Scaffolding Projects

As math teachers invite students to create in-depth representations of their solutions or thinking, they realize that this work may require more time than a single class period. Think about your workshop, then, as a fractal, each day a workshop within a greater workshop.

For examples, math teachers at Amarillo's Tascosa High School decided to invite students to create projects demonstrating their understanding of systems of equations. Each group was expected to create a poster with several different elements: a story, equations, tables, graphs, explanations, all aesthetically pleasing. Teachers learned that instead of explaining the task Monday and leaving learners alone to work each day until time to present on Friday, students were more successful when each day was a focused workshop, one for each phase of the task, for example:

Monday—story and equation

Tuesday—graphing

Wednesday—explanation

Thursday—poster assembly

Friday—presentation skills.

Each daily workshop can include examining an exemplary product, a discussion of what quality looks like, brainstorming of the steps one might take to attain that quality, as well as clear expectations for daily work time. In this way, each day's workshop builds toward the larger project goal, like a play within a play. After this closely scaffolded experience, teachers hope that learners will be more confident and prepared for greater measures of independence on their next project.

their own understanding of the concept at hand through a process that makes sense to them, with the resources and support that they need. This is an example of differentiation by learning process.

Differentiation is a critical approach to ensuring that all learners have purposeful and meaningful work to do during a minds-on math workshop. So, after you select your task for the day, think carefully about your learners and what they will need to gain a foothold and sustain motivation as mathematicians during the work time. This sort of advanced planning can make the difference between concentration and confusion.

Planning the Groups for Work Time

Once you know what learners are going to be doing, what scaffolds and systems of differentiation you will put in place, you need to consider how learners will be grouped. I have never worked with a team of math teachers who did not ask this question: How do I group students? Setting up groups starts with establishing classroom norms and a positive community of learners from day one, as described in Chapter 4. Each workshop thereafter builds upon and feeds that culture of thinking.

Grouping Strategies One critical step in putting learners together in groups is deciding which group size best suits the task at hand. Avoid determining group size based on availability of supplies or furniture arrangement, and instead look at what you want learners to do and consider how many might be actively engaged together to complete the task. Too often, I observe groups of five grappling with a problem students could tackle in twos or threes. Keeping groups small (twos, threes, occasionally fours for complex, multifaceted tasks) increases both engagement and accountability.

But what you really want to know is *who* to put together into that group of three. There are many schools of thought on this, but we do know that keeping homogeneous groups to a minimum ensures that no learner gets trapped in a "fixed" mindset, believing that she is and will remain a bluebird forever left behind by the soaring eagles at the front table.

Whatever grouping method you choose, as you match students, you might consider

- math competence—how successfully students grasp the content
- math confidence—how efficacious learners feel as mathematicians
- language background—which languages students speak, and how proficiently they speak English
- gender
- behavior—how well students collaborate.

You could spend a lot of time with color-coded sticky notes strategically placing each learner in an appropriate cluster of peers, though as soon as the chemistry is just right, invariably the wind will turn, and your best-crafted group can go astray. Instead of overthinking group assignments, I recommend that you consider the following principles, allow some randomness, and be prepared to change groups often.

- Culturally and linguistically diverse learners with limited English proficiency will thrive when they have at least one native-language peer with whom to confer.
- When students with very high or very low achievement and/or confidence levels are placed in the same group, it can be difficult for the historical underachiever to learn from and participate in the conversation.
- Oil and water don't mix. Why distract from everyone's learning by placing students with patterns of conflict in the same group?

Given those principles, you need to decide how much control you want to retain over the composition of groups each time you switch. Here are some approaches you might employ, depending upon how involved you want to be.

- Assign groups by careful planning: Based on the principles noted earlier, sit down and decide who should work with whom. But beware: Students know when they are being assigned to the bluebirds, the eagles, or the struggling sparrows, and we want to embrace the growth mindset and avoid the Pygmalion effect to the greatest extent possible. Similarly, I would dispense with the philosophy of putting "one high achiever, two middle, and one low" in each group. Students can look around the table and see right through that one and make instantaneous decisions about how they will behave: Let Sophie do all the work.

- Appointment clock: One of my colleagues loves the appointment clock—he gave each student a sheet with lines at each hour and invited them to gather into groups of twos and threes and sign up on each others' clock. It takes time to set up the first day, but then throughout the year, he could say, "Everyone meet your ten o'clock partner!" Students had had a chance to pick a friend already and could simply refer to their appointment calendar (pasted in the front of their notebooks) and know who to work with.

- Card partners: Stack a deck of cards so that the number of cards is equal to the number of students in the class and so that each card has a partner (black two with black two; red jack with red jack). Then, deal the cards, and let students find their partners.

- Random: Put every student's name on an index card. Right in front of them, shuffle the cards, stick them on the wall in a pocket chart. That's the seating chart, and those are the groups, no engineering, no favors, no exceptions. When I used this system, I'd tell my students that in life they are not going to get to choose their colleagues, and that right here right now is the time to practice working with everyone.

Supporting Group Work Chapter 5 details numerous examples of the ways in which we can support learners in succeeding as members of collaborative groups. In grouping students and asking them to think and learn together, we are not only enhancing their math learning but also inviting them to develop the twenty-first-century skill of collaboration. This is an ongoing process, not something that can be taught in September, then left alone. Students need constant reminders to reinforce why we are working in groups, how it ought to look and sound, and that part of the learning can be frustrating yet that as growth-minded mathematicians, we can solve those problems together.

So, when Sage came to me complaining about working with Angel, rather than jump in and re-set her group, I might say, "Yah, it can be really tough to collaborate. And it is one of the most important things you can learn in life. So, what are you going to do to work this out with Angel?" Although I stood at the ready to intervene as needed, I knew my role was to facilitate and support, not to take away the problems of group work. Learners develop problem-solving skills by solving problems—social or mathematical.

Figure 8.1 *Work completed alone can reveal the depth of students' understanding.*

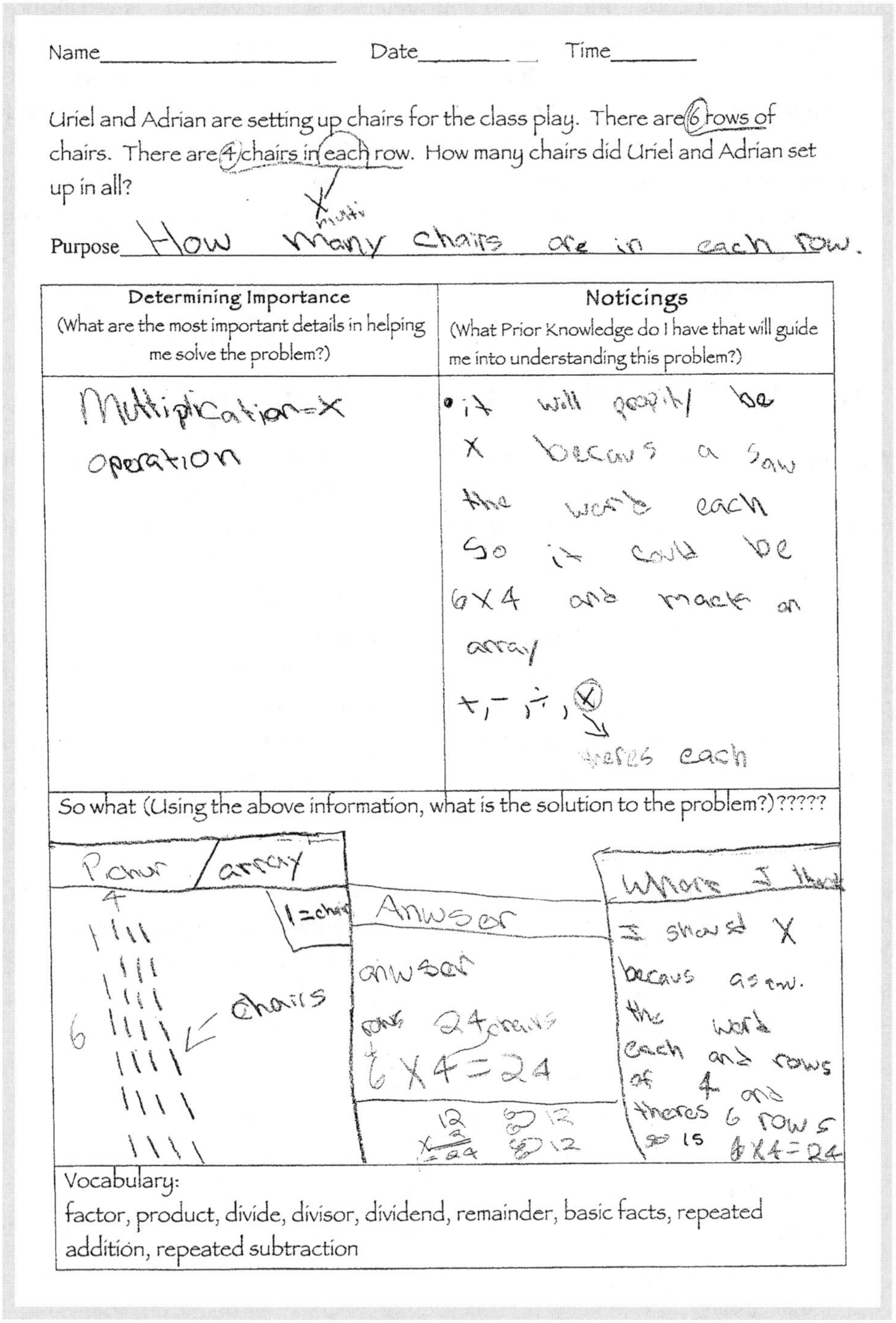

Name_____ Date_____ Time_____

Uriel and Adrian are setting up chairs for the class play. There are 6 rows of chairs. There are 4 chairs in each row. How many chairs did Uriel and Adrian set up in all?

Purpose __How many chairs are in each row.__

Determining Importance (What are the most important details in helping me solve the problem?)	Noticings (What Prior Knowledge do I have that will guide me into understanding this problem?)
Multiplication=X operation	• it will poobily be X becaus a saw the word each So it could be 6X4 and make an array +, −, ÷, ⊗ ↓ yeres each

So what (Using the above information, what is the solution to the problem?)?????

P.chur / array
4
||||
|||
|||| 1=chair   Answser
6 |||| ← chairs   anwser
|||| ans 24 chairs
|||| 6X4=24
|||| 12 812
|||| ×2 812
|||| =24

Whore I think
I shows X becaus as tw. the word each and rows of 4 and theres 6 rows so is 6X4=24

Vocabulary:
factor, product, divide, divisor, dividend, remainder, basic facts, repeated addition, repeated subtraction

Time to Work Alone Although group work is a wonderful tool, there are also times to have students work alone. Some teachers start a task this way—inviting students to read it over and get going by themselves so that they have some thinking to bring to a group conversation. Other teachers like to allow students to discuss a problem and work toward a solution together, then to go on in silence and let individuals write about what they understand. You need to find your own rhythm with this. The principle is that through collaboration students can learn a great deal, but that their learning needs to be their own, and so within each workshop, we can create time for independence, perhaps with the warm-up, or before launching a group task, or during the reflection time. In this way, students have opportunities to anchor their own thinking before or after engaging in conversations.

The Work of Work Time: Students

Work time works when learners work. Ideally, over time, we prepare students for independence by teaching the growth mindset (Chapter 1), building a positive learning community (Chapter 4), and rehearsing and reflecting upon the skills of academic discourse (Chapter 5).

So, now they are ready: Learners work when they know what they are supposed to do and why and how. You have carefully planned the task, the structure around the task, and the purpose and learning goals you are after. To actualize your careful planning, after your minilesson, the transition to work time needs to convey these three critical messages—the what, why, and how—to learners explicitly, orally, and in writing, with examples as necessary, and followed by a check for understanding.

What to Do

Based on your learning goals for the group and your formative assessment, you get to select the work of work time. This might include students working individually or in small groups exploring curricular materials from your school's math program, delving into juicy tasks you've introduced (see Chapter 3), clarifying conceptual understanding with synthesis activities, or some combination of all of these. For example, during work time, learners might:

- generate questions about the topic of the upcoming unit
- wrestle to solve one juicy problem in a table group, record their thinking, then work independently on some practice problems
- work independently to complete a problem or problem set from the text, document their thinking, then shift to sharing and discussing their work with a small group

- work with a partner to create a concept map (see Synthesis in Math sidebar) that clarifies the relationship between important unit vocabulary terms.

Most teachers I visit assign specific tasks—finish section 3.2 and 3.3, or complete both sides of the worksheet—during work time, yet few at the middle grades stop to unpack what "finish" or "complete" ought to look like. It only takes a minute to slip a page of student work under the document camera and do a quick peer critique, "What do you notice about this learner's work?" From this simple question can emerge a fruitful conversation about how finished work should look: legible, neat, labeled, accurate, with units, and so forth.

We get what we ask for from students, and so taking a moment, frequently, to be clear about what we are asking for is well worth the investment, lest quality slip. All learners need to dive into work time knowing exactly what they need to bring back toward the close of class.

In addition to being clear about their primary task, we also need to ensure that there is no "done," that students have additional responsibilities to attend to if they complete the assigned math workshop task in the time allowed: These may include additional practice, supporting others, reading about math, or practicing basic skills games.

In describing how students ought to proceed, we can refer them to the strategy modeled in that day's minilesson, as well as make connections to previous minilessons, clarifying how they might approach their task, what materials are available, who they will work with, where they will work, and any other details that need to be explicit.

Synthesis in Math

Synthesis is the act of growing your thinking, noticing how your new learning connects to prior knowledge. Concept mapping is one way for learners to gather and synthesize what they know about a given topic. Concept mapping is appropriate before, during, and after a learning activity—as a preassessment or the review of a unit.

Before creating a concept map, teacher and students need to create a list of important words or ideas to be synthesized. For beginning concept mappers, it is easier to start with a large piece of paper and a small-tipped pen or pencil for optimal legibility of the final product. For example, if we were embarking on a study of data analysis, our preassessment concept map could include somewhat familiar terms: average, mean, median, mode, outlier, range. How students are able to connect and explain these words is a window into their prior knowledge about the topic at hand.

To create a concept map like this, each word or idea is placed in a circle and a line is drawn to connect it to related words or ideas. Along the line, students explain the connection in their own words, in as much detail as possible. It works best to explain each connection before drawing the next line to avoid ending up with a wordless sketch of a spider. Figure 8.3 shows a sample concept map.

While mapping, learners may elect to add additional words or concepts in circles of their own to help make the connections stronger. This task invites learners to put ideas together for themselves, synthesizing important learning.

Figure 8.2 *Showing thoughtfully completed student work helps other learners understand what "finished" work looks like.*

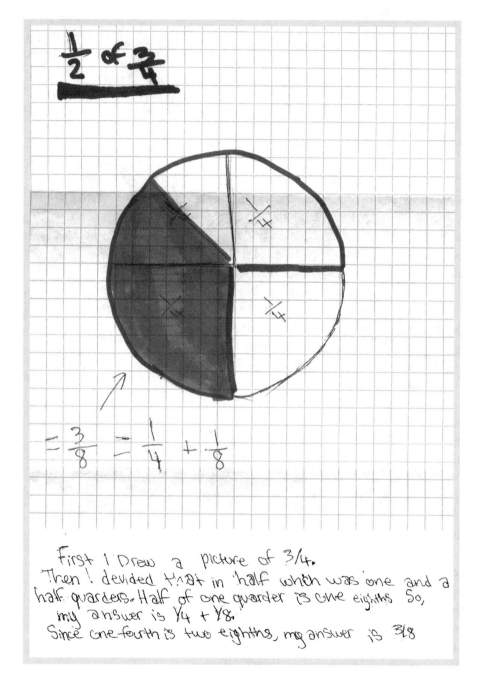

Figure 8.3

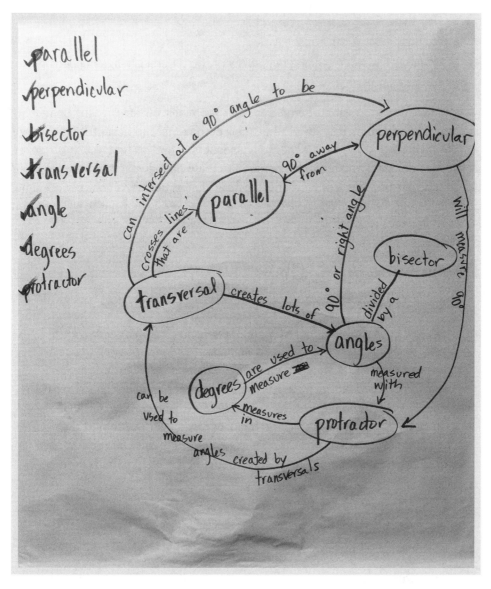

Why to Do It

More important than neat and complete is that learners actually generate understanding as they work. "What are you up to?" I often lean over and ask a student as they work in math class.

What might you hope your students would say?

a. "Finishing 3.2."

b. "Getting ready for the quiz."

c. "Working on understanding probability of two different things happening."

d. "Waiting for the bell."

My hope for you is that learners in your room will be able to say something like "c" every day, that they know what their purpose is and accept the challenge as growth-minded standards-based self-assessors. That is, that you have so effectively established and conveyed purpose to them during your opening, explained the connection between purpose and the task during the transition to work time, that they remain continuously conscious of why they are doing what they have been asked to do.

Transition to Work Time

So, let's put all that together. What could this transition sound like?

> "So, we've just talked about how mathematicians use mental models to solve problems, and that there is an infinite number of possible models one could develop. Today, you are going to be applying that strategy to your work on probability. Your goal is to really develop your understanding of how to find the chances of two different things happening—like rolling the same number twice on a die, or pulling out the same color ball twice from a collection. To do this, I want you to show me your mental model for each situation. What are some of the mental models we have used?"

> "Tree diagrams."

> "Drawings."

> "With blocks."

> "Pie pictures."

> "Fractions."

> "Good, so you know a lot of ways to make a mental model. And you get to decide which format you use for each question. At the end of our work time, when we come back together, everyone needs to bring with them not only the solutions to the practice problems, but also their mental models clearly labeled so that we can all understand your good thinking.

What questions do you have about your responsibilities today?"

After answering questions, the teacher asks students to turn and talk, explain to a partner the what, why, and how of this work time. Then, she warm calls on a few people to state it aloud to the whole group. Once everyone is clear, she releases them to get started working with a partner. "Today, you will work with your shoulder partner on this task, though each of you may decide to create or sketch different models. How loud do you think our voices will need to be in order to do this?"

Spending a few minutes explicitly stating the what, why, and how of a task—rather than simply assigning a page—can be time-consuming, but this is time well spent when it ensures that all learners dive into work time with a clarity of direction and purpose.

The Work of Work Time: Teachers

Like a canoeing instructor who has at last launched all of her paddling students on a mission around a distant buoy and now stands alone in the silence on the dock, I can be tempted to lean back during the work time to enjoy the view. But our work is not done; our role simply changes. As students get down to work, it becomes our responsibility to promote thinking, gather data, and, in some measure, to troubleshoot.

You may be accustomed to a different role, one of monitoring students' behavior. The truth is, when we make it a priority to police the classroom rather than engage in conversations with learners about their thinking, we send the message that our primary role is manager of behavior rather than facilitator of mathematical insight.

Promoting Thinking

Conferring is the go-to strategy for a teacher during work time: This is your chance to get nose to nose with learners and deepen your understanding of how they think, what they need, and where they have grown. In the next chapter, conferring will be described and explored in greater detail, but for now, consider it your primary job during work time to sit with learners and learn about their mathematical thinking.

Gathering Data

In addition to being a strategy for promoting thinking, conferring is also an opportunity for gathering data. As we confer with individuals and small groups, we can track the kinds of additional support students seem to need, find new and interesting ways to think about problems and ideas, as well as track teams' work through the lens of tools or community, as discussed in Chapters 2 and 4, respectively.

Data gathered during work time is critical fodder for planning. If we notice that students share a common confusion about what happens to a decimal point in a multiplication problem, we may elect to devote additional learning time to just that concept in the coming week. Alternately, if we observe students blazing through a task with little effort, this could be an indicator that we need to adjust the level of rigor in our next lesson. Observing and noting students' preparedness and confidence as they proceed provides the responsive teacher critical data for decision making.

Another sort of data we may gather as students buckle down to work is the range of approaches teams may use as problem solvers: Some may be drawing the mathematical situation, others modeling with Unifix cubes, and still a third group may choose to act things out. These various approaches are useful and interesting to discuss in the sharing time, so we may visit with those groups and briefly check in with them. "I love how you are thinking about this. Would you be willing to share that with the whole group when we come back together?" Seeding the sharing in this way ensures that a variety of voices and perspectives are presented when the class reconvenes to report.

A third kind of data you might gather would be about students' progress toward the embedded skills you are working toward all year long: twenty-first-century skills including collaboration and discourse, thinking strategies, Common Core standards, and so forth. You may elect to track students' agility with one aspect at a time to both report back to learners as well as to inform your instruction.

Troubleshooting

Invariably, as learners get going, some will encounter snags. When these arise, we need to make good decisions about when to get involved and when to refer learners to their own resources. When we do insert ourselves, we can consciously intervene in ways that support students' agency and efficacy. Depending on the issue, it may be appropriate to troubleshoot with one or two individuals, to gather a small group, or to press pause on the progress of the entire class to clarify a point.

Inefficiency Although to the greatest extent possible we want to resist the temptation to police and cajole during work time, we can address learners head-on when we observe their efficiency waning. I recently overheard one such conversation between Rachel and a pair of her students:

"How did you feel about your work yesterday? Was it your very best fourth-grade work? Did you get a lot done?" The students look down sheepishly.

"No."

"Your stamina was low. I noticed that. What can I do to help you with your stamina today so that you can get the job done?"

One boy shrugs, signaling that he is unsure, and the other is silent.

"Should I focus you on a couple of boxes [problems] to work on? Would that help?"

He nods, and Rachel leans across to his math page and circles two of the six boxes with her marker. *"Start with whichever one you want, but get both of these done,"* she clarifies her expectation, then reaches over to the second boy's page and circles the same ones.

"What should you do if you get stuck?" Ms. Rosenberg asks before leaving the boys.

"Call you," one offers.

"You could call me, but what else could you do? What tools do you have in this room?"

"Calculator," suggests a boy.

"Background knowledge," adds the other.

Rachel jumps on this: *"That's the most important tool! I did that today. Remember. . . ."* (She reminds the students how during the minilesson she herself relied on background knowledge to solve a problem.)

"What other tools?" she invites the students to brainstorm more possible strategies for moving over speed bumps in their productivity.

"Manipulatives?"

She affirms, *"We have blocks, walls, posters. Can you go up and use those? Yes you can! You can work together, but you must finish. And I am telling you now,"* she puts in gently, *"this is wrong."* She points to one answer. *"So go back and figure out why it's wrong and what you have to do. I'll be back."*

Through this conversation, Rachel reemphasized her expectations for each individual's craftsmanship as a mathematician, reminded them of the abundance of resources available for their use, and reinforced her expectations for their independence.

Stuck When learners get stumped, they often want help. To the extent that we help them by giving answers and fixing up their confusion, we create dependence. Instead, in our roles as facilitators of thinking, we can address their questions with questions of our own. You might ask:

- What do you understand?

- Where did you lose your way?

- What have you tried?

- What questions do you have?

- What resources might help you?

- What are you hoping I can tell you?

- What strategies have helped you in the past when you got stuck?

- What are you going to do now?

There are many charms to answering a student's question with a question. Most importantly, learners come to realize that you are not going to tell them answers but instead invite them to clarify and deepen their own thinking. The point is not to frustrate students, but rather to back up to a time when they were clear and then scaffold their thinking from there, with questions rather than answers and directions. Once you do this enough times, learners realize that you are not going to let them off the hook, so they may as well work harder at thinking for themselves.

Invitational Groups When you notice that several students have common questions or that you seem to be observing similar sources of confusion in a couple of teams, you can always call those students together at a table and talk through the work with them. Some teachers do this right away: As they release the class to work time, they may invite students who need additional support or who want to see further examples to stay close and get started together. This can be a wonderful strategy for differentiation as long as those who stay for the group are eventually released to work independently and do not get stuck thinking that the teacher's knee is the only place for them.

Catch and Release Most effective implementers of workshop model instruction use what Sam Bennett (2007) referred to as a "catch and release," a quick break in the action where a teacher gathers everyone's attention to deliver some information.

The catch can be an accolade for the great work underway, with reference to a specific team or strategy. "Wow! You all are off to a fantastic start here. I love how

I see so many different strategies emerging to make sense of this problem. Liza's team has rulers and graph paper. Raul and his group decided to get a calculator to work with the large numbers; and I am looking forward to seeing what Jerome and his friends decide." This sort of commentary highlights effective students at work and presents options to those who have not yet found direction.

A catch could also be used to deliver a tidbit of information that will be helpful to learners as they proceed: "As I see you all working, I notice every group is trying to find the y-intercept to graph the equation. That will definitely work. And, it is hard to do sometimes. What other ways do you know for figuring out how to plot a line on a graph?" A few hands shoot into the air. The teacher calls on no one. "You have ideas! Tell them to your group, and try them out," she encourages.

A catch can also be a reminder of the expectations of product or process: "We have been working so hard for twenty minutes on this task, and we only have five more minutes before we come back together. Remember that what you need to bring with you is not only your solution but also a narrative description of why you think it's right. Each person on your team needs to have their own writing to share."

Catch and release is a simple, flexible system for keeping positive momentum going during the work of work time.

Accountability What if, despite your exquisite efforts to design and facilitate an exemplary minds-on math workshop, students don't buy it? What if they don't work? At this point, so many teachers are accustomed to pulling out the stick (consequences), but better still is to try the carrot. We can offer some:

- Encouragement: "Keep up the effort."

- Reminders: "Last time you got stuck, you worked so hard and figured things out."

- Principles: "Mathematicians need stamina."

- Training: "Mental muscles get stronger when we exercise them."

- Empathy: "I struggle myself and know how it feels."

- Interdependence: "We are all looking forward to learning how you figure this out."

- Confidence: "You can do it!"

- Responsibility: "You are responsible for your own learning and for supporting the learning of others."

In the moment, we are sometimes taxed and trying everything to get an unmotivated learner moving. This has happened to all of us. At times like those, we may be tempted to blame the students, but truly the only thing we have power to change is ourselves. Best to reflect upon our own practice and how we can adjust to increase students' investment. Consider:

- What do learners need?

- How could I make the purpose more clear?

- How could I break the task into more accessible bites?

- How could I demonstrate the relevance or importance of this learning?

- How could I make this more interesting?

- What did students perceive as the consequences for not doing this?

- How can I build bridges with those students who are opting out?

For workshops to work, we all need to be clear about what we are doing and how and why. Learners need to know their responsibilities, and teachers need to devote their time to promoting thinking.

"Yeah, but . . ."

"Students get mad when I don't just tell them the answers."

If students are accustomed to teachers "helping" by giving answers, they will indeed feel frustrated if you respond to their questions with questions. Let them know why you are doing this, that your goal is to promote their good thinking, and that you want to see them succeed. It is a culture change, and it may take time, but when we give in and do tell answers, we suggest to students, "No need for you to think—if you wait me out, I will let you off the hook."

"Students complain that they can't work with certain partners."

In the past, students may have been unsuccessful with certain peers, so we do need to encourage them to recognize how this learning they are about to embark on will be different. They need to develop some go-to strategies for when they get stuck as a group (see Chapter 5). Let them know that you need them to give it a try, to talk about what goes well and what doesn't, and to learn through this experience about collaboration.

"My students never finish in the time I give them."

So often, I have observed tasks expand into the time allotted: We give students ten minutes, and they beg for more, so we stretch to twelve, then fifteen . . . as the time expands, productivity can decline. Although we want to support all learners' success by allowing them the minutes they need, we can enhance learners' focus and productivity by creating urgency, using shorter spurts of work time (with catch and release) with clear expectations and checkpoints, rather than letting them languish in casual conversation for protracted chunks of time.

Quod Erat Demonstrandum

To cultivate student independence, teachers need to set learners up for success with quality minilessons and clear direction, as well as challenging tasks that can motivate and engage. Teachers need to prepare for work time by making wise decisions about differentiation and student groupings. During work time, learners are responsible for doing their own thinking, solving their own problems, and collaborating successfully with peers while their teacher confers and gathers data.

CHAPTER 9

Conferring

Nobody sees a flower—really—it is so small. It takes time—we haven't time—and to see takes time, like to have a friend takes time.

—*Georgia O'Keeffe,* **Georgia O'Keeffe: One Hundred Flowers**

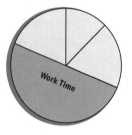

Problem of the Day: How can you get to know your students individually as math learners, promote their confidence and growth?

Postulate: While students are working independently or in small groups, teachers can assess and promote thinking and communication skills by engaging in individual conversations about mathematical understanding.

> "Isabella, sit down."
>
> "What are you doing, Ava? Four times six, remember, what's four times six?"
>
> "Eighteen?"
>
> "Eighteen?! Try again."
>
> "Um . . . twenty-four?"
>
> "Good, now write that down before you forget."

Too often, this is what math class sounds like: teachers telling learners what to do. After being told what to do long enough, some students start to believe that they themselves do not know what to do and must wait for a rescue by a smart teacher. Conferring is not about telling learners what to do or rescuing students from thinking: To confer is to intentionally create opportunities to honor learners' ideas by listening and learning alongside them.

In this chapter, I will describe how to confer, when and where to confer, as well as how to set up systems and structures that support your conferring routines.

Teacher Voices

All day long, teachers talk with students. As I described in Chapter 5, recently I spent time listening in on student talk, then tallying all the teacher–student exchanges I heard. Nearly all of those adult–learner conversations fit into predictable categories; here they are in order from most to least common:

- Policing, as in, "What are you supposed to be doing right now, James? I said stay with your group. You are not the materials manager. Go back to your desk."

- Directing, as in, "Take out a piece of paper, open your books to page 89, and look up at me when you are ready to move on."

- Accounting, as in, "My grade book says that only fourteen people turned in their homework this week. There are twenty-six of you in here. What do you think this is going to do to your grades?"

- Correcting, as in, "A square *is* a rhombus, a special rhombus, but still a rhombus! A rhombus has four equal sides. Think about it."

- Rescuing, as in, "No, four times seven is twenty-eight! Go back and fix up your answer to number eleven."

- Socializing, as in, "I heard you guys won last night! Congratulations! I hope to make it to your next game. When is it?"

- Praising, as in, "Thank you, table three, for getting your materials ready. I can see that you are prepared for our next activity."

What does this say about how the adults in that building choose to play their roles as teachers? The way we interact with students, through every conversation, informs their perception of their own identity as mathematicians, as well as their understanding of what learning is supposed to look like in math class. For this reason, it is imperative that we intentionally commit the majority of classroom conversations to thoughtful, respectful exchanges about mathematical ideas. Conferring is a key forum for conveying to learners our deep respect for their thinking.

What Conferring Is and Why It Matters

When students are *finally* working independently, we can be tempted to turn our attention to other seemingly pressing affairs: attendance, emails, grading, paperwork. But when we do so, we miss golden opportunities to focus in on individuals and support their thinking and understanding, our most important role as teachers. There are always so many tasks in a teacher's inbox that we can find it difficult to see the forest for the trees—yet, it is the *learning* not the paperwork that matters most in school.

Within a minds-on math workshop, a teacher's role changes from that of lecturer to that of coach. When a soccer coach is teaching players to kick with the outside of their foot, she can watch and see who has mastered that skill, who needs further assistance, and what kinds of additional support may be helpful. Thinking, unlike soccer moves, is often invisible. Conferring is a key opportunity for a teacher to unveil how a learner comprehends a concept, what gaps may be troubling her, and how to move her to the next level of understanding.

> *A room full of seventh graders is tilted over their graph paper, finding the areas of composite shapes. A quiet hum of conversation fills the air, but there is a palpable hush in the room. At first glance, their teacher is nowhere to be seen, but upon closer inspection, she can be found crouched down, nestled between two learners at their table as they discuss number three.*
>
> *"So, what are you thinking?" the teacher asks.*
>
> *"We got different answers."*
>
> *"Tell me more."*
>
> *"Well, I divided it into two rectangles and a triangle, and I got 162 square meters. Will did it differently, and he got something different."*
>
> *"Will?"*
>
> *"I made it a rectangle, a parallelogram, and a triangle," Will explains.*
>
> *"Mm."*
>
> *"And we didn't get the same answer."*
>
> *Pause.*
>
> *"What do you think about that?"*
>
> *"I think either way could be right," Will offers.*
>
> *"Could this shape have two different areas?" the teacher inquires.*

"No, there can only be one right area, but I think you can divide it up into any shapes and still get the same answer as long as you count all the areas right."

"But we didn't get the same," Aldo points out. "Maybe we did the math part wrong."

"Hmm. So, what could you do?"

"Do it again?"

"Let's both try doing it each other's way."

"And what would that tell you?"

"Well, if we get the same answer doing it the same way, then we are probably right."

"So, Aldo, does it matter how you divide up the figure?" their teacher checks.

"No, I mean, as long as you add up all the smaller areas to get the total area, you should get the same answer."

"So is there just one right way to solve this problem, Will?"

"Well, it will be right if you count all the boxes, but how you count them— like, in which chunks—doesn't really matter."

"So, your method and Aldo's method should both work?"

"As long as we do the calculations part right."

"Great! I like the idea of you both using each other's strategies and seeing if you get the same answer. Give that a try, and let me know what you find out."

The teacher slips over to the next table and kneels between another pair of thinkers as Aldo and Will get to work.

This is what conferring sounds like: honest inquiry into mathematical thinking. Conferring is four parts listening, and one part instruction. To confer is to sit eye to eye with a learner, listen, strive to understand what that student is thinking, and find ways to nudge the learner's understanding forward. The most important takeaway messages students should receive from a conferring experience include:

- You are a capable mathematician.

- I, your teacher, am here to support you but not to take away the struggle.

- I, your teacher, care about you as a thinker and communicator.

Through conferring, we can deliver these messages regularly and individually to all of the students in our classes, forming important relationships and building students' confidence in their abilities to explain ideas.

Understanding individual students as learners takes deliberate time and effort. Yet, if we commit the time and energy necessary for establishing conferring routines, skillful questioning techniques, cultivating patience to listen, and a classroom culture that supports us in doing so, we will create wonderful and unique opportunities to

- know students well as learners
- support students' developing communication skills
- intervene on the spot when confusion or misconceptions arise
- maintain high levels of student motivation and engagement in our classes
- coach learners toward independent success, and
- individualize and differentiate instruction.

Sometimes the harried nature of a school day can leave us feeling like we are battling our way through a forest without taking the time to acquaint ourselves with the individual trees. Conferring can be a breath of fresh air, a daily ritual that invites and allows us to connect with our true purpose as teachers—to catch learners being brilliant.

How to Confer

As a college student, I worked several summers at a wilderness camp, and I remember my boss once conferring with me as I attempted to sharpen a chain saw.

"So, what are you doing there, Wend?" Ron asked.

"Sharpening the saw."

"And, how is it going?"

"Okay."

"Show me how you are doing it." I did.

"Take a look at that saw. Which way do the teeth go when it's running?" I pointed with my finger.

"So, which edge do you think needs to be the sharpest? Which direction should you be running the file?"

Maybe you have never sharpened a chain saw, but there are a lot of ways to do it wrong, and I had landed upon one of them. Yet, through this conversation, I was led to recognize the folly of my strategy and to adjust, with understanding. Not only did I learn how to sharpen the saw, but I learned how to think through the correct filing direction the next time I forgot it. Ron's stance of coaching me to uncover my own error was a stroke of brilliance I as a classroom teacher later strove to emulate.

Although many teachers engage in individual conversations with learners throughout a day's lessons, too often we are trapped in the typical pattern of helping that leaves students dependent and awaiting our approval. Let's take a look in the table below at how conferring differs.

Many times, when I have "taught" conferring to groups of teachers, they remain hesitant to try it, concerned that they will not know what to ask, or will do it "wrong." The truth is, there is no wrong way to confer, as long as you keep your focus on students sharing their thinking! Unfortunately, few students have

TYPICAL "HELPING" VERSUS CONFERRING

	Typical Helping	**Intentional Conferring**
Focus	Ensure student gets correct answer.	Inquire about student's thinking and comprehension.
Students' role	Listen. Ask questions.	Explain thinking.
Teacher's role	Explain. Note mistakes.	Listen. Ask questions.
Outcome	Student gets correct answer.	Student hones problem solving strategies. Teacher understands student as thinker.
Inferred beliefs	Teacher is repository of knowledge, dispensing answers to students.	Students are capable problem solvers with interesting ideas to share.

Conferring Supports English Language Learners

Conferring creates opportunities for students to share their thinking one-on-one, an ideal chance for learners to rehearse putting their ideas into words. As research on second language learners suggests, sheltered opportunities to practice academic language are critical to language acquisition. Some teachers, after conferring, invite students to present an idea from their conversation with the class during the closing sharing; this builds learners' confidence.

Conferring can also present an opportunity to introduce or reinforce important unit vocabulary and ensure that students understand the terms being used in class. Once students grasp the terminology, they can begin to utilize academic language more often to explain their thinking to peers as well as to the whole group.

By supporting students' use of vocabulary and creating opportunities for learners to practice thinking aloud, conferring promotes the development of students' communication skills.

an adult in their lives who will sit with them for three to five minutes and just listen to what they are thinking. Your time and attention in and of themselves communicate to learners your confidence and the hope you hold that they will have wonderful ideas to share.

Here are some guidelines to get you started.

When and Where

Conferring works best during student work time. While the entire class is engaged in some form of small group or individual work, you can strategically commit some minutes of your time to connect with individuals.

Meeting students where they are—at their table or desk—and talking about what they are working on, the very thing in front of them, works great. You may also bring with you recent assessments, or problems you'd like to hear them think through, depending upon what you as the teacher are interested in learning from these students. Bring a chair so you can meet at eye level.

You might confer with learners individually or in small groups, depending upon what your students are working on at the time. When your goal is to support a student in mastering a specific skill that may be of concern, individual conferring works best. Yet when students are working in small groups on tasks that require interdependence, it makes more sense to chat with an entire group at once.

Some teachers may elect to call students over to another table to confer or to discuss another task or topic at this time, both of which can work. Yet, conferring routines work best when they create minimal disruption in students' work flow. That is, when your students feel like your conversation is a part of the work they were already doing before you arrived and that they can easily and smoothly return to independence when you move on.

Start small. Two to five minutes are enough to confer. As you begin, you may only get to one or two students per period. This is okay. These visits will soon start to add up.

What to Talk About

Conferring as a practice was developed by literacy teachers as a means to monitor students' unique thinking and understanding as they read and write, yet it is readily adaptable into any field of learning. Most frameworks describing conferring—and there are many developed by literacy specialists from Patrick Allen to Carl Anderson— recommend a three-step approach:

- Research—Find out what the learner knows and is thinking.
- Coach—Nudge the learner forward with one specific point of instruction.
- Reflect/record—Ask the learner what she now understands as a result of your interaction, and then document the conversation.

Research In the first minute, your job is to find out where the student is as a learner right now. You probably already have some data based on classroom participation and formative assessment, but still, take a minute to observe and interview as you get started. Your data gathering may include listening in on a learner's conversation with peers, observing his work with manipulatives, reading what he has written, and interviewing him about his thinking. At this stage, resist the temptation to correct or instruct—just study the learner and his learning for a few moments.

> The story problem is about a leopard leaping after a gazelle. The leopard leaps six meters with each stride. The gazelle has a twenty-meter head start and is advancing only three meters with each stride. The problem suggests that they are taking strides at the same rate.
>
> A pair of students is translating this word problem into an algebraic equation they have written 3g = 6 l. You ask them to describe their thinking, and one explains, "For the gazelle it's three meters for every step and for the leopard it's six, so their steps are equal."

Time to coach.

Coach After gathering data, a coaching point may crystallize quickly in your mind— or perhaps there are a number of things this learner needs to know to move forward. Pick one. Probe to learn what the student really does or does not understand about the concept you have identified.

Then, coach briefly: Ask questions, explain, model, demonstrate, write notes and examples on a sheet of paper the learner can keep. Your goal here is not to feed a man a fish—that, as we know, only creates dependence—but instead to teach him to fish: Walk the learner through the thinking required to solve this and similar problems, just as Ron taught me how to think about my chain saw–sharpening technique.

> *"So, you are right that each animal travels a different distance per jump. But what are we really trying to figure out here?"*
>
> *"Where they meet up."*
>
> *"So, how are we going to do that?"*
>
> *"You have to know how fast they're going."*
>
> *"Good, and you have that a gazelle jumps three meters each time, while the leopard jumps six. Anything else we need?"*
>
> *"Oh! The starting point, where they are."*
>
> *"What is the gazelle's starting point?"*
>
> *"Twenty meters." She points to her drawing.*
>
> *"Good, so then what do we need?"*
>
> *"We need the three, the distance she travels with each stride."*
>
> *"Three meters."*
>
> *"So, how can you say that algebraically?"*
>
> *"Hmm, twenty is the beginning, so then I guess three is what we multiply by the number of strides . . . so, it's, um, 20 + 3s."*
>
> *"Can you write that? And can you draw lines connecting your equation to parts of your sketch above?"*
>
> *"Nice, and what does that 3s + 20 equal?"*
>
> *"How far she goes."*
>
> *"What will you call that?"*
>
> *"D for distance. So, d = 3s + 20."*

Reflect/Record Before you go, take a moment to lean back together from the task at hand. Talk with the student about what she learned and what she needs to remember and how. Jot notes for yourself about the conversation so that you have a record. Encourage the learner to keep up the great work as you depart.

> *"So, what do you think of d = 3s + 20?"*
>
> *"Well, that seems right because 20 is where she started, then three more meters for every leap."*

"So, what did we do?"

"We found the starting point and the thing that changed."

"How did that help you to write an equation?"

"The starting place is just a number, but the measurement per leap, that is the thing you have to multiply."

"And the d?"

"That's what it all equals up to, the distance."

"So, what is it you need to remember for next time?"

"Find the starting place and then the rate things change."

"You got it!" You jot a note on your clipboard and move on.

Classroom Management That Supports Conferring

This all sounds great, right?! Peaceful moments ogling over one young mathematician's rendition of Pascal's triangle while the rest of the class silently chugs along. Your classroom conditions may already be conducive to conferring, yet for some teachers, some groundwork is necessary before students are collectively prepared to support this routine. How can you get started?

- Explain what you are doing and why.
- Articulate and uphold expectations.
- Give real feedback.

Let's take those one at a time.

Explain what you are doing and why.

Unfortunately, some learners spend their lives in classrooms where the teachers' main roles are as police officers and accountants. For these young people, the

---

Some Conferring Questions

Research. Try one or more of the following:

- Tell me about what you are doing.
- How's it going?
- Show me a problem you liked solving.
- How does this work?
- Wow! How did you do that?
- What's up?

Coach. Try one or more of the following:

- Show me what you understand in a picture.
- Explain to me what parts you do understand.
- What questions do you have?
- Can you remember any similar problems and how you solved those?
- What would help look like?

Reflect/record. Try one or more of the following:

- What was important to remember about solving this problem?
- What do you need to remember?
- How did this conversation help you?
- How has your thinking changed?

notion that you want to spend time talking with individuals about their thinking may be new. Explain the goals of conferring in terms they can understand. It might sound like this: "I want to get to know each of you as a mathematician and to create opportunities for you to share your ideas with me. The best way to do that is to spend some time talking with each of you, one-on-one. I am going to do this during class time, so that will mean that while I am conferring with one of you, the rest of the class is going to need to take responsibility for their own learning. If you can be in charge of yourselves while I am talking with Xavier, then Lucy, then Ben, trust me, your turn will come, and your classmates will do the same for you."

Now, there may be some students who are not really into this. They prefer the idea of poking themselves in the eye with a pencil to talking with their math teacher about math. This is only because they have not yet done either. You may need to work to win them over, and so those first conversations they overhear in your classroom need to be as affirming as possible so that everyone eavesdropping feels good and is secretly thinking, "Hey, I want him to come and sit with me and say those kind things."

Students will soon come to learn that you are not coming around to police them but rather to learn about them as thinkers. Still, you may need to explain more than once your conferring hopes and rationale.

Articulate and uphold expectations.

"Unless you are bleeding or vomiting, don't interrupt" is the rule when Rachel Rosenberg is conferring. The thing about conferring is that it can only happen if you make it a priority, higher than paperwork, teen drama, or even policing other students' behavior. It can be very difficult to force ourselves to devote this type of attention to students one at a time, and it can be harder still for the rest of the class to let us. They want to know if they can go to the bathroom. They want to borrow a pencil. They see Clayton texting under his coat, or Myra feeding pencil shavings to the class pet. So, if you are serious about making time for conferring, you need to set the expectations high: Do what you are supposed to do. Don't interrupt. Ever.

Now, there will probably be problems. The first time you sit down with Trey to talk about distance, rate, and time, Simone is going to explode and do her level best to get you involved in an argument with Eliza about the blue eraser. At this point, you have an important decision to make: Which of the following do you choose?

  a. Ignore the girls and stick with Trey.
  b. Interrupt briefly, separate the arguers, and then resume your conversation.
  c. Give up, deciding this class is just not ready for conferring.
  d. Cash in your airline miles on a trip to the Bahamas and depart immediately.

I hope that you choose a or b. Conferring takes effort and practice. With dogged determination, you can train your classes to cooperate and allow this important routine to be a staple of your culture.

Give real feedback.

Now, here's the thing: After you are done talking with Trey (assuming you got back to him and did not leave for the airport), you have a great opportunity to be real with your students. Share how you felt about being interrupted. Invite Trey to share how he felt. Re-explain why conferring is important to you. Discuss again what the class can do to make conferring possible. Talk about the specific incident and brainstorm possible solutions the girls could have employed when things got heated. Affirm that you know the class can do better next time.

By keeping it real in this way, we communicate to students that we are aware of their behavior and its effects on our classroom culture, that we know they can do better, and that this is what we expect. As you can imagine, getting students onboard takes time, will power, and sophisticated negotiation, but in the end it will be well worth the struggle when you see the positive culture of learning evolve in your classroom. (For more ideas on wrangling students' investment in their own learning community, see Chapter 4.)

Time for Everyone

If you are like me, you were already doing the math a few pages ago: Okay, so I have thirty-four students in my class, and our work time might be up to thirty minutes, so then let's say I finally get up to speed on this and can use twenty of those minutes for five-minute conferences, that is four a day, say four days a week, so sixteen a week (if we have a regular schedule and everyone cooperates), so it will take me more than two weeks to talk to each kid. What is the point of that?

Well, there is a lot of point. First of all, conferring with even one student sends a message to the whole class: I see you as individual learners, and I care about your thinking. Also, as conferring routines are established, it gets easier. You may be able to connect with six or eight kids in those same twenty minutes because you become more efficient and learners know what to expect.

And, although it is important to connect with everyone in the class, the reality is that some students need us more than others. As Rick Wormeli so aptly titled his book, *Fair Isn't Always Equal* (2006). We may need to confer more frequently with some learners than others. Some conferences may be longer than others. But if we keep track of whom we've talked to, keep everyone on our radar, and do our level best, we will surprisingly find the time for everyone.

But start small. Set manageable goals—one student per math period for the first week, then stretch from there.

Record Keeping

Conferring offers us so much data that we would be remiss not to keep some sort of record of these conversations. There are many different approaches to this, and you will need to select the one that works best for you. Here are some ideas:

- *Class list on a clipboard*. Some teachers keep clipboards with fresh class lists each time they start a new unit. Each time they confer, they make a quick note of the topic next to that student's name on the list. They hang onto the list until they have seen everyone at least once, then file it and start a new one. See Figure 9.1 for a sample conferring log template.

- *Table groups*. In a notebook or on a clipboard, teachers can sketch the layout of the classroom and identify who is at each table. After conferring at a table, they jot who they talked with and what was discussed.

- *Individual student files*. Other teachers keep a file on each individual student with a log in there of each conferring conversation. Though tracking this paperwork may be more cumbersome, it allows more space for note keeping and an easier system for accessing information on an individual as needed for meetings and conferences.

- *Emails*. These days many of our students have email, so we can also keep notes electronically by sending students brief summaries of our conferring conversations: "Gopal, It was great talking with you today about exponents. You clearly understand the power of a power. I appreciate that you asked the question about why anything to the zero-eth is one. That confused me for a long time, too. Did you have a chance to explain what we talked about to your dad?" This way, the student gets a reminder of the conversation, and you also have a record in your Sent box. Of course, to be able to do this, you will need to either bring a laptop to the conversation or jot notes while conferring to email later.

Conferring is hard work and takes time. Yet, when we commit ourselves to knowing students well and dedicate our class time to coaching and teaching mathematical thinkers, conferring needs to be an integral part of our daily routine.

Figure 9.1

SAMPLE CONFERRING RECORD

Name and Date	Research	Coach	Reflect

"Yeah, but . . ."

"I can't get the rest of the class to stay on task while I confer!"

They might not. Despite your very best efforts to motivate and monitor, other students may lose focus while you are conferring. But, think about it: You are only sitting still for three minutes, then you can go back and check up on the other learners and reignite their interest in their work. This is a small price to pay for changing your job description from taskmaster to ally.

"I never know what to ask."

You can start with the questions in this chapter, carry them on your clipboard, try them on, or make up others that may work better for you. Many teachers I know have just two or three pat questions that they repeat over and over, "How's it going? What are you thinking? How can you be so sure?" Trust yourself. Talking with a student one-on-one need not be any more intimidating than standing up in front of a whole group. Even if you just listen and wait, you may be surprised what a student might say.

"What if other kids are listening?"

What a terrific problem to have! So, I am sitting with Michael discussing the order of operations and clearing up his confusions about the acronym PEMDAS; Tonya overhears us from the next table, recognizes that she is similarly confused, so stops her work to eavesdrop on our conversation. What a great use of everyone's time!

Quod Erat Demonstrandum

Conferring provides teachers with key opportunities to listen to students' thinking, understand their strengths and challenges, and address individual learners' needs. A typical conferring conversation includes three parts—research, coach, and record—and takes place in just a few minutes while other class members are working. Classroom routines that support conferring take work to establish, and conferring, like any skill, takes effort and practice. Yet if our goals are to honor individual learners and their thinking, to cultivate their communication skills, and to hone our ability to differentiate instruction, conferring is well worth the investment.

CHAPTER **10**

Sharing and Reflection

*The highest reward for a person's toil is not what he gets for it
but what he becomes by it.*

—John Ruskin

Problem of the Day: How can we ensure that students end class understanding and retaining their learning?

Postulate: To remember and reapply what they learn, students need opportunities to share their thinking, respond to the thinking of others, and consider how their ideas have changed and grown.

On the first day of a new unit, a well-prepared sixth-grade teacher shows students some graphs from that morning's newspaper displaying mortgage rates over time, and the number of new home construction projects started each month. With these, she invites learners to consider a new concept: independent and dependent variables. As soon as the words leave her lips, a student exclaims, "We did this last year."

Other students chime in, "Yah, we did this a whole bunch in math and science both."

"Did you?" Surprised, their teacher wants to know more. "So, what do you remember about independent and dependent variables?"

"I don't know. We just did them."

There is a distinct difference between *doing* and *learning*, though these experiences can be symbiotic. The thinking process that accompanies the task ensures that learning will result from doing the task. Some students are automatically and constantly monitoring their own thinking, integrating new ideas into prior knowledge, and adjusting their understanding with each experience. Yet all benefit from intentional opportunities to solidify comprehension at regular intervals. This is why the last segment of a workshop—sharing and reflection—is the most important. In fact, unless we punctuate our lesson with some opportunity for metacognition, much learning is lost.

If we are to pursue conceptual understanding of important ideas as described by the Common Core State Standards, we must create these regular opportunities for learners to solidify their comprehension, as well as hone their agility with mathematical practices.

Metacognition—thinking about our own thinking—is a critical step in learning; it is also a learned skill. Metacognition gives students an opportunity to synthesize their understanding, monitor their own progress, and focus their intention for the days to come. Sharing and reflection time also provides a teacher with important data to guide her planning in the days to come. As we close our workshops, we need to intentionally save time for all learners to have the opportunity to reference their good work back to their understanding goals.

Constantly pressed for time and stressed by expectations for coverage, math teachers can be reluctant to devote precious minutes to these moments that don't involve students "doing" math. But if we want learners to really *understand* the math they are doing, and we want to understand what they understand, we need to give ourselves as a community of learners this gift of time to think about our own thinking. Otherwise, we are trying to put a second coat of paint on the walls without letting the first coat dry.

In this chapter, I describe why metacognition is important and how to invite students to share—to communicate their understanding and collaboratively deepen their thinking—as well as how to invite learners to reflect—to think about their own thinking. I describe a range of strategies for each as well as scaffolds to support students' successful engagement. Taking time for these often-skipped opportunities will ensure that students leave our classrooms able to say not only that they *did* independent and dependent variables but, more importantly, that they *learned* exactly what that concept means.

The Importance of Metacognition

As described in Chapter 6, in their meta-analysis *How People Learn*, The National Research Council (2000) identified three factors that promote learning:

- engaging preconceptions
- offering learners a conceptual framework, and finally
- creating opportunities for metacognition

Sharing and reflection time directly addresses this third factor. About the value of metacognition, the authors state in their later volume, *How Students Learn*,

> Appropriate kinds of self-monitoring and reflection have been demonstrated to support learning with understanding in a variety of areas. In one study [Aleven and Koedinger 2002], for example, students who were directed to engage in self-explanation as they solved mathematics problems developed deeper conceptual understanding than did students who solved those same problems but did not engage in self-explanation. This was true even though the common time limitation on both groups meant that the self-explaining students solved fewer problems in total. (2005, 11)

As students share, they are challenged to articulate their own process as problem solvers; as they listen to peers explain, learners consider how another's thinking matches up with or diverges from their own. During reflection, a student steps back from her own work as a mathematician and notices how her thinking has changed. Sharing and reflection, though distinct from one another, achieve the common purpose of promoting metacognition.

Of course we can encourage students' metacognition—awareness of their own process, thinking, and understanding—throughout an entire workshop. Yet the closing rituals of sharing and reflection specifically structure in an opportunity for each learner to have a daily dose of self-awareness.

Let's listen in as Deb Maruyama wraps up a class by inviting learners to share and reflect on what they know about exponents at the close of a work time reading activity introducing exponential notation as a way to document population growth in a shorthand form:

Ms. Maruyama: *So, what is an exponent?*

Sadie: *An exponent is when you want to break down a multiplication problem that has the same factor.*

Elisa: *It's a quantity expressed by a number.*

Julia: *It's a string of factors—the number that's being multiplied more than once—it's a string of the same factor being multiplied more than once.*

Ms. Maruyama: *You're saying that it's 2 × 2 × 2 × 2 × 2?*

Julia: *That factor that's being used more than once is the base.*

Jack [whispering]: *Say, "It's a simpler form."*

Joleen: *Exponential form is a simpler form to write a long string of products that have the same factor being multiplied more than once.*

Ms. Maruyama: *So we've got to incorporate Julia's, Joleen's, Elisa's, and Sadie's ideas. Who can help?*

Sadie: *Exponential form is the shortcut to writing a long string of the same factor multiplied more than once.*

Pascal: *The factor being used more than once is the base, and how many times the factor's being multiplied is the exponent.*

Ms. Maruyama: *Nice job. I know that this took a long time. But you'll get better at this. Nice job thinking. Outstanding.*

Next, Ms. Maruyama asks students to take out their notebooks and do some writing about what they understand. She gives them a sentence frame:

> Today I was trying to focus on connections between. . . . So I . . . and figured out that in the future I can find unknown vocabulary definitions in text by. . . .

Here, Deb models beautifully how a group oral sharing opportunity, followed by individual written reflection, need not take up too much time. Though you may feel initially reluctant to make this investment of time as you close your minds-on math workshop, the payoffs in student understanding, teacher understanding of student thinking, and opportunities for assessment are well worth the time. In fact, some math teachers claim that reflection is the most important thing they do with learners, partly because it is also helpful as a source of formative assessment data that can guide their planning.

Sharing as Metacognition

The purpose of sharing is to invite students to consider their own ideas and solutions, but also to evaluate their thinking in light of that of their peers. The goal is not to identify who got something "right" and who got it "wrong." Sharing is a time to celebrate the multiple approaches that might lead to a shared, accurate understanding, as well as to explore misconceptions or common errors that could get in a mathematician's way. Through sharing, we all get smarter about the meaning of mathematics.

Let's take a look at some structures for sharing, as well as the means to scaffold students' successful participation in this ritual.

Structures for Sharing

You can organize students in many ways to get together and talk about their work.

Presentations to the Whole Group Most commonly, teachers invite learners to share their thinking and artifacts of their work before the entire class. This is a great forum for engaging all in effective discourse about the topic at hand. Some students may eagerly and confidently approach the document camera to project their work; others may be more reluctant. You can "seed" the sharing by

TYPICAL "CORRECTING" VERSUS MINDS-ON SHARING

	Typical "Correcting"	Minds on Sharing
Focus on	◆ Answers	◆ The thinking behind the solutions
Students' role	◆ Figuring out if they got it "right"	◆ Understanding the ideas of peers ◆ Reconsidering their own approach and solution
Teachers' role	◆ Assessing who is correct ◆ Correcting mistakes	◆ Probing for deeper explanations ◆ Inviting thinking by listeners ◆ Gathering data on students' needs
Role of errors	◆ Corrected by telling right answers	◆ Explored to uncover and address the thinking that led that problem solver astray

inviting individuals during conferring time and encouraging them to share their good thinking with the group when everyone comes back together.

Once student presenters have the mic, honor the individual or team by expecting and allowing them to do their own explaining, even if it takes time, even if their language is imprecise, and even if they have made errors. Let them speak for themselves. Probe the group with questions as needed, turning the clarification over to the learners. For more ideas on facilitating discourse of this nature, see Chapter 5.

On a recent visit to Rachel Rosenberg's room, I observed her sitting patiently among the class while one student struggled at the SMART Board to articulate his thinking:

> **Ms. Rosenberg:** *What is the mode?*
>
> **Zar:** *The mode is three because the most students walk three blocks.*
>
> **Ms. Rosenberg:** *Sonia, do you agree or disagree with Zar?*
> *[Long pause.]*
>
> **Sonia:** *I agree with Zar because . . . Ms. Rosenberg, I don't understand.*
> *[She looks back at her teacher.]*
>
> **Ms. Rosenberg:** *Ms. Rosenberg's not talking, so who do you need to talk to? Talk to Zar. It's not about me.*
> *[Sonia looks back up at the student at the board.]*
>
> **Zar:** *Like three, it's the one that has the most, not the most blocks, but the most people that walk those blocks. [He points to the graph on the SMART Board and counts.] Four people walk three blocks. That's the most.*

To prepare students for conversations like these, we need to regularly explain, model, and reflect on how mathematicians talk with one another, how we can each explain our thinking. Ms. Rosenberg has explicitly taught her students to follow their answers with *because*, then to respond to peers thinking with the sentence stem, "I agree with so and so because. . . ." These conversational phrases, though simple, need to be explicitly taught. See Chapter 5 on discourse for more ideas on sentence stems you might teach learners to use during sharing time.

When students share, we may find ourselves tempted to jump in, to seize their pen or pencil, or even silence their voices so that we can—to our minds—more clearly describe their solution. This usurping of the microphone only suggests that we do not believe learners are up for the job of explaining their thinking. But this is something they must learn, and the only way they will learn is to model and discuss our expectations: middle school teacher Brad Smith will himself demonstrate to the class two ways to go to the board: one silent, the other with an explanation of thinking. Then, they discuss which was most useful to the audience.

Tracey Shaw invites learners to begin sharing from their seats after working on an algebraic equation describing how to calculate the cost of a group trip to a math fair:

Ms. Shaw: *I know you may not be completely done with the graph, but can I get a couple groups to share what you came up with as an equation? What are you thinking? What should the cost be if ten students go?*

Rose: *One hundred seventy.*

Ms. Shaw: *Anyone else get that?*

Lizzy: *We got that.*

John: *We got 125.*

Ms. Shaw: *Okay, let's hear your thinking, Rose. How did you get 170?*

Rose: *Okay, so for ours, our first equation was y = 1200/x + 5, but then we realized that would only be adding $5 to the total cost, and you need to add $5 per student. So our second equation was y = 1200/x + 5x.*

Ms. Shaw: *So somebody that got 125, explain your thinking.*

John: *The problem is just telling you to add $5 to the cost per student adding on to the original from problem two, so that's how I got 125. So, I think I can figure out: with the 170, it's saying each student is paying 170. With the 125, it's saying each student is paying 125.*

Here you see Ms. Shaw resisting the temptation to rescue students by declaring which solution is correct and instead allowing them time to wrestle through their own explanations. This conversation continued for some time, as she artfully engaged learners in the Common Core's third mathematical practice: construct viable arguments and critique the reasoning of others. She values this process for all learners and allows time for them to ask each other questions until they can collectively make sense of a situation. This commitment to allowing time for learners to think is far more effective in surfacing misconceptions and confusion than any answer sheet we might hand out.

If you do choose this forum for sharing, you may only have time to hear from a few teams on a given day. That is all right—not everyone needs to present their ideas at each opportunity, but do keep track, lest T. J. imagine that he can be spared this opportunity.

Pairs or Trios The virtue of whole-group sharing sessions is that we as the teacher can monitor and think with the class as a group. But only a few students get turns to talk. Thus, to increase conversational opportunities, we may want to invite learners to share in pairs or trios comprised of partners who did not spend the work time learning together.

To set up these small groups, all students need to have their own artifacts from their work time in hand to talk about, and we need to establish expectations for volume and participation and give explicit instructions for what learners are to talk about.

To group students quickly, we can simply invite them to grab their face partner, shoulder partner, someone wearing the same color top or similar shoes, or someone they have not talked with yet that day—you probably already have your own strategies for grouping learners quickly. We could even invite learners to go back to back with their partners (as modeled by Mr. Dennis in Chapter 6). Directions might include: From today's work, share . . .

- how you used your background knowledge to help you

- one thing you are sure about, and one that you are unsure of

- something you feel proud of figuring out

- what you did and what you are thinking now

- the questions you are still wondering about.

Keep the time short, lest learners veer into other conversations. As you crisply call the group back together, you can practice some warm calling (see Chapter 5), demonstrating to all your clear expectation that they use that sharing time to really talk about the question at hand.

This structure is useful after an in-depth project or even a juicy problem-solving session as a format for generating discussion and conversation. Your questions could be those from the previous section or might include broader ones, such as:

- Describe what your group did.

- Describe your work and why you think it is correct.

- Describe two ways you could have solved the problem.

- Describe what you have accomplished and what you plan to do next.

This format could also work for a peer critique, giving learners a chance to give peers feedback on work in progress.

Gallery Walk Picture this: hushed students meandering around the classroom, reading, writing, thinking about the mathematical reasoning of their peers. This is what occurs during a gallery walk: Students post their work, whether completed posters, charts, graphs, or other tasks, either completed or in progress. All learners have a few sticky notes and a pencil, and their job is to amble through the classroom, reading and reviewing the work, then to jot comments on sticky notes and leave those on or near each piece. You might start by giving learners just three sticky notes each and allowing them to choose the work to critique or compliment. This all occurs in the same silent mood one might experience while viewing the Mona Lisa.

For students to give and receive productive feedback during a gallery walk, it is helpful to first spend time talking about how to give good feedback: Be specific, sincere, and compassionate. "Nice job," for example, is far less helpful than, "Nice job labeling your axes with titles and units." Or, "Why did you decide it was a linear function?" is far more evocative than, "Huh?" If we want learners to develop their ability to construct and critique arguments, they can be each other's mentors and coaches, expecting that peers explain their solutions and ideas in ways that make logical sense. We will need to model and discuss the sorts of questions and comments that best serve this purpose.

Scaffolding Students' Participation

Sharing in all its myriad forms goes best when learners understand the what, the why, and the how of their task. Take time before launching a sharing session, large or small, to remind students of the norms of your learning community and the goal of supporting one another in getting smarter together. To that end, invite all to experience and rehearse the procedure for sharing—whether orally or in writing—to ensure that the classroom remains a safe place for everyone's ideas. If the conversation or tone begins to go astray, leap in as though your hair is on fire. You cannot risk allowing learners to shut one another down. Everyone's mind needs to be on.

To this end, I often strike an empathetic chord with my students, inviting them to consider how they wanted to be treated when they shared their ideas, and reminding them of the golden rule and its important place in our classroom.

Reflection

While sharing is the process of presenting one's own thinking and learning from the thinking of others, reflection involves considering one's own progress, one's own growth as a mathematician. It is that walk on the beach with your dad when he asks you how you are and really means it. It's what teacher Deb Maruyama calls the "So what?" of the lesson.

Similar to sharing, though distinct, reflection is learners' opportunity to step back from their work and that of their peers and to consider what their work means, why it matters, and what they learned about themselves as thinkers that day. Reflection might be about the content, the process, or both; it could be about behavior or skills or standards, though probably not all at once. The purpose of reflection is quite simply to invite learners to look in the mirror at themselves and their group and to consider what they have accomplished and its significance.

Structures for Reflection

You might invite students to reflect at various intervals over the course of a project. Daily reflection is valuable, and then many teachers pause at the end of a unit or semester to invite students to look more in depth at their progress as learners.

Learners can reflect orally with the whole group, in small groups, in pairs, or in writing in a variety of formats: on small whiteboards, on sticky notes, in math journals, on the back of today's work, on a tracker listing the learning goals, or simply on a special sheet of paper. This written reflection could serve as your exit ticket for any given day.

At the close of class investigating operations with positive and negative numbers, Brad Smith invites, "You just taught yourselves the rules for multiplying and dividing positive and negative numbers. Now in your journal, you need to synthesize these rules for yourselves. How would you describe them? Put this title in your journal [on screen]: Rules for Multiplying and Dividing with Positives and Negatives. We're going to take what we just shared and turn it into rules." Then, learners end class with some silent writing time.

Reflection Prompts

Here are some ideas of what to ask:

- How has your thinking solidified or changed?
- What patterns have you noticed?
- Share one thing you learned from another mathematician.
- What was your biggest "aha" moment today?
- What questions do you have about what you learned today?
- What is the most important thing you want to remember?
- Write about something you wish we had more time to investigate.

- Tell of one thing you understand; one you are still confused about.
- Give feedback for the teacher about how today's class could have been even better.
- What will you say when your friends ask you, "What was math class about today?"
- If we were starting class with a pop quiz tomorrow, what would the questions be?
- What do you think we are going to do next?
- How did you use your background knowledge today?
- What was important about today's lesson?
- I used to think _____. Now, I think _____.
- What? So what? Now what?

Scaffolding Students' Reflection Writing

In inviting students to write thorough reflections, Deb Maruyama says to them, "Pretend like you're talking to me, and write that down. Think of all the questions I could ask. Be specific enough that I don't ask those questions."

As with any piece of writing, learners need to know their purpose and audience and to understand the elements of good communication: specific language and clear explanations. You will need to show models and critique examples together to generate a shared understanding of expectations for quality. Reflection writing is a genre itself and merits some time and attention if you would like students to write well and completely as mathematicians.

Figure 10.1

Today I learned that if I only had one angle mesure I could find the rest. I could do this because I know what angles on the diagram that are congruent. I also know that each Line is a straight angle and straight angles are 180° so if the Line is split and I know what one side is I would subtract the side I knew from 180° which would give me the other sides measurment.

Getting Kids to Write

♦ Establish purpose; describe the power of nonfiction writing to boost academic achievement, as articulated by Douglas Reeves in his research on 90/90/90 schools (2000).

♦ Debunk students' belief that math is "not about writing" by showing them models of professional mathematicians' work: Einstein, Descartes, Euclid, Fibonacci, and others.

♦ Model your own writing process by thinking aloud as you compose a model reflection.

♦ Give learners feedback immediately during writing time; confer. "Say more," you might kneel down and prompt an individual whose piece appears pithy. "Help me understand what you know about the distributive property."

♦ Frequently share samples of completed student work and discuss as a group whether they meet standards of quality. You can use work from another class and have names taken off, if that feels more appropriate.

♦ Consistently dedicate sufficient class time to writing so that it is not rushed or blown off.

♦ Co-create and post a chart or rubric listing descriptors of quality for math writing.

Take time to show and discuss examples of what you expect and to talk about the value of clear written communication. Also, find ways to respond to students' reflections, whether in writing or simply through whole-class or individual conversations. If you are going to ask them to write, take the time to read.

Though for the purpose of this chapter, I am isolating sharing and reflection from one another, you are probably noticing the many ways in which they could and should overlap in this final segment of the workshop.

Tracking Data

One purpose of all of this sharing and reflection is to promote learners' understanding of what they do and do not yet comprehend, to focus their growth-minded minds on what they need to go after next as learners. Equally important is that you seize these opportunities to gather data on how students are thinking about the content, what they need, and what kind of support will catalyze their development as mathematicians.

As you listen to students share, perk up your ears for trends and needs:

• Are learners grasping the meaning behind the numbers?

• Are learners referring to the big ideas represented in this unit?

• Are students able to estimate and know whether answers are reasonable?

• Are learners precise with their arithmetic?

• Are students understanding and using content vocabulary accurately and with fluency?

• Are learners embracing a variety of strategies and models, or sticking with one?

SAMPLE RUBRIC FOR WRITTEN MATHEMATICAL EXPLANATIONS

	1	3	5
		(All of 1, Plus . . .)	(All of 3, Plus . . .)
Mathematical accuracy	◆ Work is completed.	◆ Work is mathematically correct.	◆ Work is organized and labeled.
Justification	◆ Answer given.	◆ Problem-solving process is described. ◆ Answer is supported with explanation.	◆ Process is described in sufficient detail that it could be replicated. ◆ Solution is represented in more than one way, including words, pictures, and numbers.
Conventions	◆ Work is legible.	◆ Work is neat and follows appropriate conventions (spelling, units, punctuation, etc.).	◆ Work is ready for publication.

These are the kinds of themes you might look for, notice, and address in an upcoming minilesson.

As with conferring, there are a variety of ways that you might track the data gathered, whether collecting anecdotal notes during classroom conversations or scouring reflections for evidence of mastery. Following are a few data collection systems you might try.

During sharing, you might collect quantitative data:

- Tally who shares their thinking with the group. (Ensure that everyone gets an opportunity eventually.)

- Tally whose sharing demonstrates mastery of the standard at hand.

- Track any widely held misconceptions (and who holds them) to be addressed in a minilesson or through conferring.

Figure 10.2 *How can we use the information from an exit slip?*

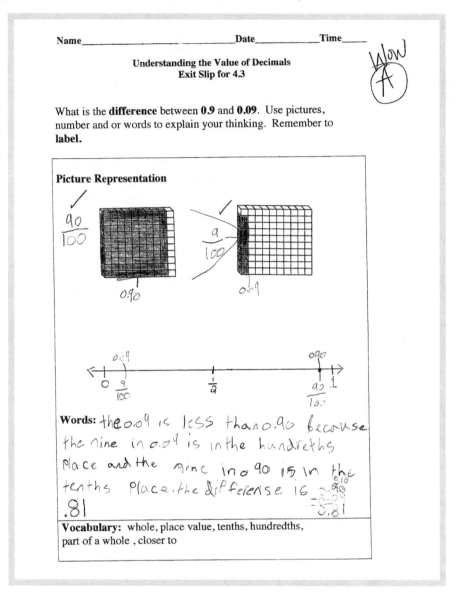

From reflections, you can collect qualitative data:

- What growth are students making?

- How confident are students feeling about this content?

- What are common areas of confusion?

- What else do learners need?

All of this formative assessment data can be used to inform your responsive teaching in the next days' and weeks' lessons. For example, if the sharing conversation reveals that several students are confused about the terms *similar* and *congruent*, you may devote additional time at the opening of the next class to invite all learners to clarify that vocabulary by looking at a series of shapes and classifying those together. Or, if on their written reflections several learners write questions about why you get to move the decimal point around when you divide, you may elect to gather them as a small group for a few minutes during the next day's work time to explore the meaning of decimals and division using manipulatives. In these ways, sharing and reflection create excellent opportunities for us to recognize and respond immediately to learners' challenges, rather than waiting for the final unit autopsy to uncover areas of confusion.

Any minds-on math workshop can offer a variety of opportunities for metacognition during the minilesson and work time, but key to ensuring students' solid grasp on their day's learning is that we pause the work time early enough to allow for sharing and reflection. Not only does this dedicated time benefit learners who are able to step back from their experience and notice their growth, but also it offers reflective teachers useful data that can inform our instruction going forward.

"Yeah, but . . . "

"This takes way too much time away from learning."

Metacognition is part of learning. When we stop to synthesize, to notice what we grasp and where our understanding has broken down, we prepare to be even more purposeful in our next learning time.

"What if students have a false sense of what they understand?"

Student overconfidence can be difficult to approach. On the one hand, we don't want to reduce their sense of efficacy as mathematicians; on the other, we want them to have an honest assessment of their strengths and needs. Try showing exemplars to students and asking them to notice the difference between their own work and the sample presented.

"I just use a quiz problem for my exit ticket."

Quiz problems can be great exit tickets, as they offer us real data on who does and does not understand how to complete a specific math task. But unless we also invite learners to talk or write or think about their work from a metacognitive standpoint, that exit ticket would not be considered a reflection. Think about how you could invite students to do both.

"How do I read all of their reflections?"

Students need not write reflections every day, and if they do, those written reflections need not be long—they could even be just a phrase or a sentence. You can quickly whip through those, sort or tally them, and get the data you need. At the close of a unit or semester, you could invite students to write longer pieces and then you may need to devote additional time to reviewing those, which you just might enjoy.

Quod Erat Demonstrandum

Research supports the value of metacognition in promoting student understanding. To that end, we can devote the final minutes of our minds-on math workshops to sharing and reflection, an opportunity not only for students to synthesize their thinking, but also for teachers to assess what students comprehend and what they need next, thus feeding the ongoing spiral of our workshops' design.

Conclusion

It is easier to build strong children than to repair broken men.
—Frederick Douglass

A young girl watches in the kitchen as her mother prepares a holiday meal: Mom pulls out a carving knife and slices half an inch off either end of a large ham before placing it in the oven. "Why did you cut the ends off, Mommy?" the child inquires.

"I don't know. That's the way my mother always did it."

Well, that answer wasn't good enough for the curious child, so later that day when Granny came to dinner, the little girl asked why it was that before putting a ham in the oven, they cut some meat off either end.

To this Granny replied, "Well, when your mother was a little girl, we had a very small oven. I had to cut the ends off the holiday ham to make it fit."

Poor mother was just copying what she had seen done for so many years, without understanding. Foolish, and yet generation to generation we have been in the habit of inviting students into the same sort of copycat behavior. The twenty-first century demands more from our children, and we have more to offer them: By engaging learners in minds-on math workshops, we invite them into a world of sense making, a land where no one makes mathematical moves because someone else said so, but rather where mathematicians approach challenges in reasonable ways. Thinking logically is a learnable skill, one we are charged to teach.

My hope for you echoes my hope for the mathematicians in your care: Don't do anything because I said so. Teach in a way that makes sense to you and, more importantly, to your students. This book is full of ideas, suggestions, examples, and models, yet it is your turn, as the master of your craft, to adopt or adapt those that best serve you and your learners.

Minds-on mathematics is not a program or a formula, but rather a stance and a challenge: design learning experiences that convey your greatest hopes for students; take them knee-deep in the work of thinking. Resist the temptation to rescue them from their toil. Confer with and coach them as they trudge through the mud and the reeds to a place of understanding. Meet them there; look back together at the trail of their thinking, and then look ahead.

Thinking Strategies for Mathematicians

	As Readers of Content *As mathematicians read reference books, textbooks, and other resources to gather information and understand mathematical ideas, they . . .*	As Problem Solvers *Mathematicians study problems in order to solve them. As problem solvers, mathematicians . . .*	As Critical Thinkers *Mathematicians evaluate their own work and the work of others. They . . .*
Ask Questions	◆ question whether concepts make sense ◆ ask how new ideas connect with prior knowledge ◆ pause and wonder about areas of confusion ◆ consider how to use new information	◆ inquire about the nature of the problem ◆ ask the purpose of the problem ◆ wonder what is the best strategies for solving ◆ inquire about potential pitfalls in the problem-solving process	◆ wonder why a solution is accurate ◆ ponder alternate approaches to the problem-solving process ◆ ask whether patterns can be generalized from special cases
Determine Importance	◆ set a purpose for their reading ◆ search for the main ideas ◆ identify important examples that help them understand ◆ select important data ◆ find special conditions or common misconceptions	◆ identify what the problem is asking ◆ select relevant data ◆ identify potential pitfalls in the problem-solving process ◆ consider special criteria that may be unique to each problem	◆ assess whether a solution addresses the purpose of the problem ◆ develop answers that make sense and are justified with mathematical reasoning ◆ correctly complete arithmetic
Draw on Background Knowledge	◆ pay attention to when they do or do not have background knowledge for a concept, and to how their background knowledge helps them to understand ◆ assess the accuracy of their background knowledge; build, revise, or delete background knowledge, as needed ◆ make connections between new ideas and concepts they already know	◆ make meaning of key vocabulary ◆ understand the type of mathematics they are being asked to do ◆ use what they know about related problems to solve new problems efficiently and accurately	◆ consider the value of mathematical applications in real-world contexts ◆ make connections between mathematical ideas ◆ build on what they already know to make sense of new mathematical situations

	As Readers of Content *As mathematicians read reference books, textbooks, and other resources to gather information and understand mathematical ideas, they . . .*	As Problem Solvers *Mathematicians study problems in order to solve them. As problem solvers, mathematicians . . .*	As Critical Thinkers *Mathematicians evaluate their own work and the work of others. They . . .*
Infer	• draw conclusions not explicitly stated in the text • generalize from specific examples	• analyze data to identify patterns • make predictions based on information given	• deduce the rationale behind a peer's work • analyze a single solution in light of a general principle
Make Mental Models	• pause to represent information and ideas in graphs, charts, drawings, diagrams, etc. • create symbolic representations that help them remember information	• organize what they know about a problem • represent abstract relationships concretely • use a variety of tools to represent a situation • develop a system for solving a problem • represent their thinking and solution	• develop and refer to models to represent their ideas • understand the thinking of others by examining their models • evaluate the effectiveness of various models in a given situation • synthesize and create new models as their understanding evolves
Monitor for Meaning	• maintain awareness of when they do and do not understand • notice confusion and stop to address it	• ensure they understand the context and situation before beginning to solve a problem • stop to classify the type of work the problem is asking them to do • estimate and then check solutions against estimates • ensure clear documentation of solutions	• explain thinking to others clearly • assess whether the thinking makes sense • inquire about the thinking of peers • attend to precision
Synthesize	• draw together various pieces of information from disparate sources • mesh new ideas with their background knowledge • notice their thinking changing over time	• generalize from patterns • match a strategy to a problem • apply concepts in new contexts • develop solutions that integrate more than one mathematical strand	• integrate their thinking with that of peers • identify commonalities between various solutions to a problem • critique the reasoning behind a solution in light of known principles • contextualize solutions within the landscape of broader principles

Resources

Juicy Problems

(Special thanks to John Ward for his contributions to this set.)

TV Shopping

You currently have an old 36" TV. Its aspect ratio (width:height) is 4:3 and there is a 2" border all around the screen. You want to buy a new TV, aspect ratio 16:9 with a 1" border around the screen. What size new TV can fit into the same space as the old TV? Width is the limiting factor.

Rabbits and Pythons

Two rabbits land on deserted Salt Island; they breed, and the number of rabbits on the island doubles every 4 weeks. Two other rabbits arrive on deserted Pepper Island; these rabbits triple every 4 weeks.

 At the end of the 12 weeks, one python arrives on each island. As each python grows, the number of rabbits it can eat each week doubles. The first week, each eats 1 rabbit, the second week, 2, and so forth. How long will it take the python to wipe out the rabbits on each island?

Pizza Choices

Alan's Pizzeria offers 7 different toppings: cheese, mushrooms, onions, olives, peppers, potatoes, and spinach. How many possible combinations of these topics could a customer order if they are allowed only "single" servings of each topping (that is, triple cheese with double onions is not an option different from cheese with onions)?

Tennis Balls

You have a cubic box full of tennis balls. They are packed so that the bottom layer is 10×10; the next layer where the balls are placed in the indents between the balls in the lower layer therefore has 9×9. Next layer 10×10, etc. If you take all the balls out and then build a pyramid on a 10×10 base inside the box, how many balls will you have left over?

Probability of PBJ

There are 10 boys and 14 girls in the class, and each has the same type of lunch box; 30% of the boys have PBJ sandwiches, as do 50% of the girls. The boxes get mixed up.

a. If you just grab one, what is the probability that you get PBJ?

b. What are the chances that you won't get a PBJ?

c. How many boxes would you have to open to be sure of getting a PBJ?

d. How would the problem need to be set up differently to give you a 40% chance of grabbing a PBJ on your first try?

Candy Choices

Your brother and you are trying to decide which box of candy bars to buy, and you have to agree on one. He thinks that flavor is the most important; you prefer to judge by appearance and you both worry about the number of calories.

You agree on a set of 3 criteria for judging the candy bars: flavor, appearance, and calories. You disagree on how much weight each of the criteria should carry.

	Flavor	Appearance	Calories
Your weighted values	25%	50%	25%
Brother's weighted values	50%	25%	25%

You do a blind taste test on 4 candy bars. Here are your scores, out of a possible 10 points.

	Flavor	Appearance	Calories
Brother's Scores			
Astrochunks	4	7	8
Besta Bite	7	8	4
Chocomania	3	5	7
Devilicious	9	2	5
Your Scores			
Astrochunks	7	9	8
Besta Bite	8	5	4
Chocomania	7	6	7
Devilicious	6	5	5

If each of you gets an equal vote, which candy should you buy a box of, and why?

Road Trip

Your family is driving from Portland, Oregon, through Canada to Anchorage, Alaska, a total of 2,557 miles, about 1,075 of which are in the U.S. If your car gets 24 miles to the gallon, and gas prices average $3.75 per gallon in the United States and $1.25 per liter in Canada, calculate the gas costs for the trip.

Transcontinental Travel

Two airplanes are flying across the country, one originating in New York, headed for Los Angeles, the other doing the opposite. The plane from New York took off at noon Eastern time and is scheduled to arrive in Los Angeles at 1:20 PM Pacific time. (Note: Pacific time + 3 hours = Eastern time.) The plane from Los Angeles departed at 10:30 Pacific time. Assuming zero wind and an identical flight path, how many hours will each flight have traveled at the time that they cross paths?

The Tortoise and the Hare

The tortoise and the hare are racing from the dale to the glen, a distance of 1008 meters. The tortoise sets off bright and early, traveling at a pace of 12 meters per minute. The hare lies in the bushes watching, knowing that she is much faster; she can hop 50 meters per minute. If the hare wants to win, what is the maximum time she can laze in the grass and watch the tortoise before getting on her way?

Greener Pastures: A Differentiated, Thematic Problem Set Including Ambiguity

> Task: Design an animal-friendly enclosure that offers livestock maximum space.

Brother Bjorn is retiring from a 29-year career as a manager of a crowded, 150-acre factory farm and has decided that he wants to spend the remainder of his days raising livestock and poultry humanely in spacious pastures. Through his years of experience, he has developed his own beliefs about the grazing land required for different species of animals. Here is a table describing his goals for ideal pasture size for his stock:

	Chickens	Cattle	Goats	Horses	Sheep	Pigs
Number per acre	50	12	20	4	10	30

Note: 1 acre = 43,560 square feet.

a. Brother Bjorn has 4 horses to accommodate. He has 1,000 yards of fencing materials and wants to build an enclosure for his newborn foal, Cupcake. He is planning to build it in the unlimited space around his 40-by-16-foot tool shed, which he will convert to a feed supply shed. In order to offer Cupcake his ideal grazing area, how much fencing will he need to use, and how much will be left over?

b. Brother Bjorn is thinking he would like to have at least 5 different kinds of animals. He definitely wants to bring in goats and name one of them Lollipop. He will build them a small pasture backed up to his 100-foot-tall cylindrical grain elevator. The grain elevator has a circumference of 150 feet. He would like to use one side of the silo as part of the goat pasture fence, to save on fencing. How much fencing will he need in order to create an enclosure large enough to accommodate ten goats with his ideal pasture area?

c. Brother Bjorn plans to house his collection of prizewinning roosters, who have earned over four dozen ribbons at the state fair over the years. To keep them each looking pristine, he would like to build a partitioned enclosure surrounding his 20-by-30-foot rectangular coop. He envisions a circular enclosure with the coop in the center, and each rooster having his own coop entrance. Design an outdoor rooster area that meets these specifications and gives each of his 9 roosters the allotted space. How much fencing will Brother Bjorn need to build it?

d. Houdini the heifer is a good milk cow but also an escape artist, so Brother Bjorn want to tether her to the outside of the barn rather than give her a pasture where she can roam free. His barn is 36 meters by 70 meters. Where on the barn should she be tethered, and what is the shortest possible rope length he can use for a tether that will afford her the ideal grazing area?

e. Priscilla the pig has just given birth to a half-dozen little piglets. This is her fourth litter. Brother Bjorn would like to keep as many of the piglets as possible and is planning to build them an enclosure surrounding the old silo, a 45-foot circumference stone structure in his north pasture near the mud hole where his former pigs liked to wallow. He has 500 feet of fencing with which to build his pig enclosure. How many piglets can he keep?

f. Brother Bjorn saw an amazingly designed circular, 24-foot-diameter sheep-shearing shed kit online that he can order for $2,200. He envisions constructing it in the middle of his rectangular sheep pasture, and then dividing his pasture into 4 equal pens, each opening directly to the shearing shed. Right now, he has a minimum pasture size for his 36 sheep. Design a way that he can add the shed, divide his grazing area into 4 equal parts, and ensure ideal pasture size for his sheep with a minimum need for additional fencing.

Note: The answers are not provided. Why not? If you could flip to the back of the book and see that you got the solution "right," you'd decide you were done and stop thinking about the problem. Without easy access to affirmation, you may ponder the problem more deeply, more fully, be tempted to discuss it longer, just to be sure you've got it. Enjoy!

Sources of Good Problems

Released Test Items

TIMSS (Trends in International Mathematics and Science Study)

http://timss.bc.edu/timss2007/items.html

http://timss.bc.edu/timss2003i/released.html

NAEP (National Assessment of Educational Progress)

http://nces.ed.gov/nationsreportcard/about/booklets.asp

CST (California State Test)

www.cde.ca.gov/ta/tg/sr/css05rtq.asp

MCAS (Massachusetts State Test)

www.doe.mass.edu/mcas/testitems.html?yr=

New York Regents Exam (via Jefferson Math Project)

www.jmap.org/JMAP_REGENTS_EXAMS.htm

Math Competitions

Canadian Open Mathematics Competition

http://cms.math.ca/Competitions/COMC/

ELMACON

www.elmacon.org/question-amp-answer-keys

Math Archives

http://archives.math.utk.edu/contests/

Independent Sources

Braided Math Extensions

www.braidedmath.com/braidedmath/Extensions.html

Khan Academy (online individualized exercises)

www.khanacademy.org/exercisedashboard

Michael Shackleford, A.S.A.

http://mathproblems.info/

Other Instructional Resources

Math Learning Center

www.mathlearningcenter.org/

Math Solutions, Marilyn Burns

www.mathsolutions.com/

NCTM (National Council of Teachers of Mathematics)

www.nctm.org/about/default.aspx?id=166

Good Books About Math

Fixx, James. 1978. *Games for the Super Intelligent.* Garden City, NY: Doubleday.
Hakim, Joy. 2007. *The Story of Science: Einstein Adds a New Dimension.* Washington, D.C.: Smithsonian Books.
Livio, Mario. 2002. *The Golden Ratio.* New York: Broadway Books.
Paulos, John Allen. 2001. *Innumeracy: Mathematical Illiteracy and Its Consequences.* New York: Hill and Wang.
Seife, Charles. 2000. *Zero: The Biography of a Dangerous Idea.* New York: Penguin.

Good Books About Teaching Math

Boaler, Jo. 2008. *What's Math Got to Do with It? Helping Children Learn to Love Their Least Favorite Subject and Why It's Important for America.* New York: Penguin.
Chapin, Suzanne. 2003. *Classroom Discussions: Using Math Talk to Help Students Learn.* Sausalito, CA: Math Solutions.

Hyde, Art. 2006. *Comprehending Math: Adapting Reading Strategies to Teach Mathematics, K–6.* Portsmouth, NH: Heinemann.

Hyde, Art, Susan Friedlander, Cheryl Heck, and Lynn Pittner. 2009. *Understanding Middle School Math: Cool Problems to Get Students Thinking and Connecting.* Portsmouth, NH: Heinemann.

Moses, Robert, and Charles E. Cobb Jr. 2001. *Radical Equations: Civil Rights from Mississippi to the Algebra Project.* Boston: Beacon Press.

Good Books About Teaching in General

Bennett, Samantha. 2007. *That Workshop Book.* Portsmouth, NH: Heinemann.

Berger, Ron. 2003. *An Ethic of Excellence.* Portsmouth, NH: Heinemann.

Dweck, Carol. 2006. *Mindset: The New Psychology of Success.* New York: Random House.

Johnston, Peter. 2004. *Choice Words: How Our Language Affects Students' Learning.* Portland, ME: Stenhouse.

Plaut, Suzanne, ed. 2009. *The Right to Literacy in Secondary Schools: Creating a Culture of Thinking.* New York: Teachers College Press.

Wiggins, Grant, and Jay McTighe. 1998. *Understanding by Design.* Alexandria, VA: ASCD.

Bibliography

Achieve the Core. www.achievethecore.org/steal-these-tools

Aleven, Vincent, and Kenneth Koedinger. 2002. "An Effective Metacognitive Strategy: Learning by Doing and Explaining with a Computer-Based Cognitive Tutor." *Cognitive Science* 26 (2): 147.

Atwell, Nancie. 1998. *In the Middle: New Understanding About Writing, Reading, and Learning.* 2d ed. Portsmouth, NH: Heinemann.

Barnes, Douglas, and Frankie Todd. 1995. *Communication and Learning Revisited: Making Meaning Through Talk.* Portsmouth, NH: Heinemann.

Bennett, Samantha. 2007. *That Workshop Book: New Systems and Structures for Classrooms That Read, Write, and Think.* Portsmouth, NH: Heinemann.

Berger, Ron. 2003. *An Ethic of Excellence.* Portsmouth, NH: Heinemann.

Bloom, B. S., M. D. Engelhart, E. J. Furst, W. H. Hill, and D. R. Krathwohl. 1956. *Taxonomy of Educational Objectives: The Classification of Educational Goals; Handbook I: Cognitive Domain.* New York: Longmans, Green.

Boaler, Jo. 2008. *What's Math Got to Do with It? Helping Children Learn to Love Their Least Favorite Subject and Why It's Important for America.* New York: Penguin.

Callaway, Nicholas. 1987. *Georgia O'Keeffe: One Hundred Flowers.* New York: Knopf.

Chapin, Suzanne. 2003. *Classroom Discussions: Using Math Talk to Help Students Learn.* Sausalito, CA: Math Solutions.

Clark, Kim. 2010a. "Can School Reform Ever Really Work?" *U.S. News & World Report* (January): 23.

———. 2010b. "The Extreme School Makeover." *U.S. News & World Report* (January): 23–27.

Cline, Foster, and Jim Fay. 2006. *Parenting with Love and Logic: Teaching Children Responsibility.* Colorado Springs, CO: NavPress.

The Conference Board, et al. 2006. "Are They Really Ready to Work? Employers' Perspectives on the Basic Knowledge and Applied Skills of New Entrants to the 21st Century Workplace." Available at www.p21.org/storage /documents/FINAL_REPORT_PDF09-29-06.pdf

Dancis, Jerome. 2010. "Alternate Learning Environment Helps Students Excel in Calculus: A Pedagogical Analysis." University of Maryland, College Park. Available at www-users.math.umd.edu/~jnd/Treisman.txt

Dweck, Carol. 2006. *Mindset: The New Psychology of Success*. New York: Random House.

Einstein, Albert. 1922. "Sidelights on Relativity." London: Methuen & Co. Available at http://en.wikiquote.org/wiki/Albert_Einstein

Flannery, Mary Ellen. 2009. "A New Look at America's English Language Learners." *NEA Today*. Available at www.nea.org/home/29160.htm#

Gonzalez, N., L. C. Moll, C. Amanti. 2005. *Funds of Knowledge: Theorizing Practices in Households, Communities and Classrooms*. Mahwah, NJ: Lawrence Erlbaum.

Graves, Donald H. 2001. *The Energy to Teach*. Portsmouth, NH: Heinemann.

Hattie, John. 2009. *Visible Learning: A Synthesis of over 800 Meta-Analyses Relating to Achievement*. New York: Routledge.

Hiebert, James. 1997. *Making Sense: Teaching and Learning Mathematics with Understanding*. Portsmouth, NH: Heinemann.

High School Survey of Student Engagement. 2005. Bloomington: Indiana University.

Hyde, Art. 2006. *Comprehending Math: Adapting Reading Strategies to Teach Mathematics, K–6*. Portsmouth, NH: Heinemann.

Hyde, Art, Susan Friedlander, Cheryl Heck, and Lynn Pittner. 2009. *Understanding Middle School Math: Cool Problems to Get Students Thinking and Connecting*. Portsmouth, NH: Heinemann.

Johnston, Peter. 2004. *Choice Words: How Our Language Affects Students' Learning*. Portland, ME: Stenhouse.

Keene, Ellin Oliver. 2008. *To Understand: New Horizons in Reading Comprehension*. Portsmouth, NH: Heinemann.

Klaus-Quinlan, Moker, and Sally Nathansen-Mejia. 2010. *Bridging Words and Worlds: Effective Instruction for Culturally & Linguistcally Diverse Learners*. Denver, CO: PEBC. Available at www.pebc.org/wp-content/uploads/2010/10/bridging-words-and-worlds.pdf

Kober, Nancy. 1993. *What We Know About Science Teaching and Learning. EdTalk*. Washington, DC: Council for Educational Development and Research. Available at www.eric.ed.gov:80/PDFS/ED361205.pdf

Kohn, Alfie. 1996. "Beyond Discipline." *Education Week* 20. Available at www.alfiekohn.org/teaching/edweek/discipline.htm

Malone, Samuel A. 2003. *Learning About Learning: An A–Z of Training and Development Tools and Techniques*. Wiltshire, UK: Cromwell Press.

Medina, John. 2008. *Brain Rules: 12 Principles for Surviving and Thriving at Work, Home, and School*. Seattle: Pear Press.

Melzer, J., and E. Hamman. 2004. *Meeting the Literacy Development Needs of Adolescent English Language Learners Through Content Area Learning*. Providence, RI: Brown University.

Merseth, Katherine. 1993. "How Old Is the Shepherd? An Essay About Mathematics Education." *Phi Delta Kappa* 74: 548–55.

Moses, Robert, and Charles E. Cobb Jr. 2001. *Radical Equations: Civil Rights from Mississippi to the Algebra Project*. Boston: Beacon Press.

National Center for Education Statistics (NCES). 2003. *TIMSS 1999 Video Study of Eighth-Grade Mathematics and Science Teaching*. Available at http://nces .ed.gov/timss/

———. 2007. *Highlights from PISA 2006: Performance of U.S. 15-Year-Old Students in Science and Mathematics Literacy in an International Context*. Available at http://nces.ed.gov/pubsearch/pubsinfo.asp?pubid=2008016

———. 2009. The Nation's Report Card: Mathematics 2009. National Assessment of Educational Progress (NAEP). Available at http://nces.ed.gov/nations reportcard/pdf/main2009/2010451.pdf

National Governors Association Center for Best Practices, Council of Chief State School Officers. 2010. Common Core State Standards in Mathematics. Washington, DC: National Governors Association Center for Best Practices, Council of Chief State School Officers. Available at www.corestandards.org /assets/CCSSI_Math%20Standards.pdf

National Research Council. 2000. *How People Learn: Brain, Mind, Experience, and School*. Washington, DC: National Academies Press.

———. 2005. *How Students Learn History, Mathematics, and Science in the Classroom*. Washington, DC: National Academies Press.

National Research Council, Committee on Increasing High School Students' Engagement and Motivation to Learn. 2004. *Engaging Schools: Fostering High School Students' Motivation to Learn*. Washington, DC: National Academies Press.

Overbaugh, Richard C., and Lynn Schultz. *Bloom's Taxonomy*. Old Dominion University. Available at www.odu.edu/educ/roverbau/Bloom/blooms_taxonomy.htm

Partnership for 21st Century Schools. 2008. *21st Century Skills, Education & Competitiveness*. Available at www.p21.org/storage/documents/21st_century _skills_education_and_competitiveness_guide.pdf

Paulos, John Allen. 2001. *Innumeracy: Mathematical Illiteracy and Its Consequences*. New York: Hill and Wang.

Pearson, P. David, and M. C. Gallagher. 1983. "The Instruction of Reading Comprehension." *Contemporary Educational Psychology* 8: 317–44.

Pearson, P. David, et al. 1992. "Developing Expertise in Reading Comprehension." In *What Research Has to Say About Reading Instruction*, edited by J. Samuels and A. Farstrup. Newark, DE: International Reading Association.

Plaut, Suzanne, ed. 2009. *The Right to Literacy in Secondary Schools: Creating a Culture of Thinking*. New York: Teachers College Press.

Quate, Stevi, and John McDermott. 2010. *Clockwatchers: Six Steps to Motivating and Engaging Disengaged Students Across the Content* Areas. Portsmouth, NH: Heinemann.

Reeves, Douglas. 2000. *Accountability in Action: A Blueprint for Learning Organizations.* Denver, CO: Advanced Learning Press.

Reinhart, Steve. 2000. "Never Say Anything a Kid Can Say." *Mathematics Teaching in the Middle School* 5 (8): 478–83. Available at www.georgiastandards.org /resources/online%20high%20school%20math%20training%20materials /math-i-session-5-never-say-anything-a-kid-can-say-article.pdf

Resnick, Lauren B., ed. 2006. "Do the Math: Cognitive Demand Makes a Difference." *Research Points* 4 (2). Available at http://hub.mspnet.org/index.cfm/14209

Ritchhart, Ron. 2002. *Intellectual Character: What It Is, Why It Matters, and How to Get It.* San Francisco: Jossey-Bass.

Roseth, C. J., D. W. Johnson, and R. T. Johnson. 2008. "Promoting Early Adolescents' Achievement and Peer Relationships: The Effect of Cooperative, Competitive, and Individualistic Goal Structures." *Psychological Bulletin* 134 (2): 223–46.

Schifter, Deborah. 2007. "What's Right About Looking at What's Wrong?" *Educational Leadership: Making Math Count* 65 (3): 22–27.

Siena, Maggie. 2009. *From Reading to Math: How Best Practices in Literacy Can Make You a Better Math Teacher.* Sausalito, CA: Math Solutions.

Sparks, Dennis. 1999. "Assessment Without Victims: An Interview with Rick Stiggins." *Journal of Staff Development* 20 (2). Available at www.learning forward.org/news/jsd/stiggins202.cfm

Stein, M. K., and S. Lane. 1996. "Instructional Tasks and the Development of Student Capacity to Think and Reason: An Analysis of the Relationship Between Teaching and Learning in a Reform Mathematics Project." *Educational Research and Evaluation* 2 (1): 50–80.

Stiggins, Richard. 1996. *Student Centered Classroom Assessment.* 2d ed. Upper Saddle River, NJ: Prentice Hall.

Tomlinson, Carol Ann, and Jay McTighe. 2006. *Integrating Differentiated Instruction and Understanding by Design.* Alexandria, VA: ASCD.

Tomlinson, Carol Ann, and Marcia B. Imbeau. 2010. *Leading and Managing a Differentiated Classroom.* Alexandria, VA: ASCD.

Van deWalle, John. A., and LouAnn H. Lovin. 2006. *Teaching Student-Centered Mathematics, Grades 5–8.* Boston, MA: Pearson.

Vygotsky, L. S. 1978. *Mind in Society: Development of Higher Psychological Processes.* Cambridge, MA: Harvard University Press.

Wagner, Tony. 2008. *The Global Achievement Gap: Why Even Our Best Schools Don't Teach the New Survival Skills Our Children Need—And What We Can Do About It.* New York: Basic Books.

Walser, Nancy. 2008. "A Conversation with Tony Wagner." Harvard Education Publishing Group. Available at www.hepg.org/blog/2

Webb, Norman L. 2002. "Depth-of-Knowledge Levels for Four Content Areas." Available at www.broward.k12.fl.us/hrd/news/docs/Depth_of_Knowledge_for_Content_Areas.pdf

Wiggins, Grant, and Jay McTighe. 1998. *Understanding by Design*. Alexandria, VA: ASCD.

Wormeli, Rick. 2006. *Fair Isn't Always Equal.* Portland, ME: Stenhouse.